George B. Loring

An Oration Delivered at Lexington

On the Dedication of the Town and Memorial Hall, April 19, 1871

George B. Loring

An Oration Delivered at Lexington
On the Dedication of the Town and Memorial Hall, April 19, 1871

ISBN/EAN: 9783337222024

Hergestellt in Europa, USA, Kanada, Australien, Japan

Cover: Foto ©ninafisch / pixelio.de

Weitere Bücher finden Sie auf **www.hansebooks.com**

AN

ORATION,

DELIVERED AT LEXINGTON ON THE

Dedication of the Town and Memorial Hall,

APRIL 19, 1871,

BEING THE

96TH ANNIVERSARY OF THE BATTLE OF LEXINGTON.

BY DR. GEORGE B. LORING.

WITH THE PROCEEDINGS AND A HISTORICAL
APPENDIX.

BOSTON:
PRESS OF T. R. MARVIN & SON,
1871.

To the Memory of

SAMUEL ADAMS. WHO INSPIRED,

AND

JOHN A. ANDREW, WHO SUSTAINED,

the heroism and devotion to freedom and humanity, which have given

Massachusetts her great name, I reverently dedicate this

Memorial of the valor of Lexington in the

two great American Wars.

ORATION.

FELLOW-CITIZENS:

NINETY-SIX years ago to-day the town of Lexington became immortal in history. The story is a familiar one. It has been recorded by the careful and patient annalist; illumined by the poet; exalted by the orator; repeated with holy zeal at the fireside; passed from tongue to tongue along all the admiring lands; and received as an inspiration by all the sons of men toiling and hoping to be free. And what a wonderful story it is! There had been great wars, and great protests; — great wars for freedom and independent nationality, great protests against tyranny and oppression. There had been great efforts, and great failures;—great efforts to establish popular government, and great failures in organizing republican states. For the diffusion of Christian light, and the freedom of Christian thought, man had risen to the sublimest heights of heroism: and, betrayed too often, had been left in the darkness of despair. The history of popular resistance was not encouraging; the history of popular effort was not in all things admirable. The clouds which gathered around aspiring humanity had been dark and heavy. The world had beheld with astonishment and admiration mingled with contempt, the dismal and tempestuous voyage of those who had launched forth upon the stormy sea of high purpose and reform. No greatness of unshaken empire, no possession of permanent power had yet rewarded the sons of revolution and revolt. There was indeed the dauntless protesting spirit, which no convulsion could extinguish, no disaster chill; there were, too, the traditions of freedom; but no more.

It was the inspiration of this defiant spirit, the natural inheritance of our fathers, of our New England fathers at least, sons of Puritans, and Separatists, and Non-conformists, recognizing amidst all surrounding events, whatever was manly, and generous, and just, and noble, which immortalized this spot. The scene, enacted here, in all its attributes, in all its significance, in all its touching associations and high quality, has not been equalled. There is a romance and sublimity about it, not woven around the old battle-fields, and the classic passes even. Its simplicity is captivating and amazing. The courage, and confidence, and faith, the untutored assurance, the absence of all art, the presence of all natural nobility, the unassuming self-assertion, displayed here—have they ever been surpassed? We are familiar with deeds of personal daring—and with the courage of heroic bands, on occasions where the exercise of heroic qualities seemed to be more natural than the exercise of meaner ones; but not with the sudden and spontaneous conversion of a small and placid community into a towering ridge of defiance, and immortal purpose, reaching to the skies.

But around this little hamlet of eight or ten families, a century ago, there was a rare accumulation of great thoughts and lofty emotions. To this little isolated community, the soundest doctrines of free society and state, civil and religious freedom, the events of American history, the breadth and strength of American humanity, the depth and wisdom of American thought, belonged by inheritance. Upon the people of this town had fallen the stern virtues, and all the hardy qualities which had been nourished by the trials and hardships which attended the founders of the American empire. These virtues were the precious freight of the Mayflower, and they had been developed and strengthened by the hard experiences of the colonists, and their descendants for many generations. By history and tradition were their minds cultivated to the highest conceptions of nationality. The familiar thought of the time was of high and solemn import. And it was the remarkable and peculiar fortune of Lexington, that to her bosom had come for safety and repose the great agitators of that day, and that her spiritual guide and light was one who "took a broad and enlightened view of the duties and obligations of the citizen."

On the night of the 18th of April, 1775, Gerry, and Orne, and Lee, had found shelter in a near and adjoining town, and Adams and

Hancock were guarded by Munroe and his brave band, at the house of the Rev. Jonas Clark, in this immediate neighborhood. Are you surprised that the custodians of such precious lives, should have baptized the cause of American freedom with their blood in the early morning? They had not forgotten, moreover, the teachings of their beloved pastor, the friend and connection of Hancock, the equal of Adams in all mental and moral qualities, who while he protected the patriots, and shared their dangers, exclaimed: — "Inspired with the principles of piety, governed by the laws of God, encouraged and supported with motives of religion, such men in the court or in the field, in peace and in war, in private and in public stations, look with a generous contempt, a sacred abhorrence upon every advantage they might make to themselves at the expense of their virtue. No self-interest, no venal motive can countervail with them the public good, the safety and happiness of society—of mankind. The powers of the great and the flatteries of the vulgar are equally despised; the greatest trials are cheerfully endured, the most self-denying services are with pleasure engaged in, in the cause of God. In honor to God they wait upon the king, in devotion to Him they serve their country, and for the glory of His name stand ready cheerfully to submit to every hardship, firmly to face every danger, and for the support of His cause, and the defence of the liberties and lives of His people, freely to make their own a sacrifice, and shed their dearest blood." Are you surprised that a pastor like this should lead a patriotic people? They remembered the words of the " noble-minded WINTHROP," when he appeared at the bar of his accusers to sustain the character and administration of Massachusetts—" Civil liberty is the proper end and object of authority, and cannot subsist without it. It is a liberty to that only which is good, just and honest. This liberty you are to stand for, with the hazard not only of your goods, but, if need be, of your lives." They remembered also that the fathers of New England by a solemn instrument, in the words of Hutchinson, " formed themselves into a proper democracy." The glowing words of Warren, just then advancing along the refulgent path which led to his martyrdom:—" I am convinced that the true spirit of liberty was never so universally diffused through all ranks and orders of men, on the face of the earth, as it now is through all North America," were uttered as a direct appeal to them. They had heard the fiery eloquence and unanswerable argument of James Otis, which, as John Adams said, " breathed into this country the breath of life." The voice of Samuel Adams was ringing in their ears, proclaiming: " We will not submit to any tax, nor become slaves. We will take up arms, and spend our last drop of blood before the King and Parliament shall impose on us, and settle crown officers in this country to dragoon us. The country was first settled by our ancestors, therefore we are free, and want no king. The times were never better in Rome than when they had no

king and were a free state; and as this is a great
empire, we shall have it in our power to give
laws to England;" spoken with a spirit of defiance which has not yet been defeated, and with
a spirit of prophecy which, as the Lord liveth,
will one day be fulfilled. And they had heard
the call of that unknown sentinel on the watch-
towers, who cried:—" If an army should be sent
to reduce us to slavery, we will put our lives in
our hands, and cry to the Judge of all the earth,
who will do right, saying: Behold, how they
come to cast us out of thy possession, which thou
hast given us to inherit. Help us, O Lord, our
God, for we rest on Thee, and in thy name we
go against this multitude! "

If we would fully appreciate the devotion and
valor which inspired these words, we should ever
bear in mind what " a feeble folk " our fathers
were, in all the attributes which constitute a state.
The population of the colonies, at the time when
they made their stand here for civil freedom,
and dreamed with Samuel Adams of American
nationality, was less than three millions; that of
Massachusetts was less than three hundred thousand: that of Boston about thirteen thousand.
The entries of foreign and coasting vessels into
the port of Boston, were about three hundred
annually, and the clearances about four hundred.
The valuation of all the property of Massachusetts, including the Province of Maine, was about
ten millions only. The travel on the great line
to New York was all more than accommodated,
(the conveyances being less crowded than at this

day,) by two stage-coaches and twelve horses. The strangers who visited Boston landed mostly at Long Wharf, we are told. Where these strangers came from we are not told. No bridges spanned the Charles or the Mystic—and none had been projected to East Boston. In Essex county, one of the oldest and most populous sections of the colony, there were only three post-offices, and the appointment of three post-masters was all the patronage of that kind which the Provincial Congress possessed. A weekly mail was a luxury; a weekly newspaper was all that the most inquisitive or ambitious could obtain for the gratification of their curiosity or ventilation of their views. The entire population of that section of Massachusetts, through which the British troops passed on their way to Concord, including a territory of five miles on either hand, was less than five thousand. The entire American army employed during the Revolutionary war which opened at Lexington, was less than twenty thousand men. And seven thousand American regulars, five thousand French troops, and four thousand militia, defeated Cornwallis at Yorktown, and secured our independence, with a loss of three hundred men. Of what our fathers had not, in these days of steam, and magnetism, and hourly mails, and half-hourly newspapers, and daily intelligence from Cathay and farthest Ind, and teeming towns, and a country populous from sea to sea, and armies flashing a million bayonets, with siege guns, which mounted on Bunker Hill, would bombard Salem on the one hand and Lexington on the other—it were vain to endeavor to tell.

It is difficult to conceive why great fleets, and the flower of the English army should have been sent to subdue a people like this—a people feeble in numbers and resources, and so reasonable in their demands upon the mother country, that the most powerful eloquence in the British Parliament was heard in their defence. But so it was: and the arrogance of man was once more employed to accomplish a divine purpose. It is not easy to understand why imposing military feints at midday, and forays at midnight, and Sunday excursions among a church-going people, should have been organized to overawe and terrify—unless the invader carried in his breast that conscience which " makes cowards of us all." And it is impossible to comprehend the reason why Leslie retreated from Salem, without firing a gun, leaving the imperial Pickering master of the field ; or why a well-armed and disciplined body of veteran troops did not pursue a triumphant and destroying way to Concord, blasting a terrified country in their march, and returning laden with the spoils of victory ; unless the manifest wickedness, and cowardice of the enterprise had paralyzed their arms. As we look back upon the repeated insults heaped upon the people of Boston, the occupation of her harbor with floating batteries, the slaughter of her citizens in her peaceful streets, the occupation of the town with strong military force, our hearts are filled with gratitude to that overruling Providence, who stayed the hands of the powerful, and converted all his efforts into the simple lesson that for the cause of freedom, "it must needs be that offences come." And we rehearse the story of those few eventful hours, which we have met to commemorate, with mingled gratitude and admiration, and with that sense of fascination, which the tale of rare adventure and great purpose always awakens.

The night of the eighteenth of April comes on, mild and soft as midsummer, and the hour approaches when the signal of conflict is to be given to a waiting American people. The hidden designs of the British governor are divulged to the officers of the British army, and the work of carrying them into operation commences. That the vigilant and watchful patriots are informed and alert is soon apparent. Joseph Warren is more than a match for Lord Percy. By the way of Roxbury he despatches William Dawes—and across the river to Charlestown he sends Paul Revere. At that moment the lights are fixed on the North Church steeple, and before a man of the British soldiery was embarked in the boats which were to convey the army to the shore of Middlesex, "the news of their coming was travelling with the rapidity of light through the country." On sped Revere, arousing the inhabitants in every hamlet and on all the wayside. He warned Adams and Hancock of their danger, at the house of Rev. Mr. Clark; roused Samuel Prescott to the work; was captured by British officers on the road, was released, and returned with renewed vigor to his rally.

Every patriot upon whose head a price had been set was placed in safety, to await the momentous events of the coming day; and in the silent watches of the night, the militia of Lexington, under Captain John Parker, assembled on this green, to scatter, after some delay, each man to his own home; and slumber settled down once more upon the silent spot. But now the morning of the nineteenth of April dawned, Wednesday morning, ninety-six years ago this day of week and month; and just before the sun appeared above the horizon, the British troops, following an advance guard, marched with quick, defiant step, into the little village, and were confronted by Parker's hastily gathered company, drawn up in battle array, — the unconscious heroes, in whose hands was placed the sublime service of firing the first shot for American freedom, and a Republic of human equality. And there they fell—Parker, and Muzzey, and Munroe, and Jonathan and Caleb Harrington, and Hadley, and Brown, the seven sons of Lexington—and Porter, the offering sent by Woburn to the sacrifice;—there they fell; and the invader passed on; the widow and the orphan remained behind; the long agony had begun. "Day came in all the beauty of an early spring. The trees were budding; the grass growing rankly a full month before its time; the blue bird and the robin gladdening the genial season, and calling forth the beams of the sun which on that morning shone with the warmth of summer; but distress and horror gathered over the inhabitants of the peaceful town. There, on the green, lay in death the gray-haired and the young; the grassy field was red with the innocent blood of their brethren slain, crying unto God for vengeance from the ground." The invader passed on to meet the men of Acton, and Concord, and Bedford, and Carlisle, and Littleton, and Chelmsford, and Reading, and Sudbury; and to be harrassed in an ignominious flight by the gathering militia from all adjoining towns. The blood of Essex mingled with that of Middlesex in the great event—and the men of Danvers lay down with the heroes of Acton, and Bedford, and Lexington, to awake to a glorious immortality. "From the nineteenth of April, 1775," said the Rev. Jonas Clark, the learned and fervent, "will be dated the liberty of the American world."

Ninety-six years have passed away, my friends, since the events I have narrated; and what a new and refulgent chapter has been added to American history in our own day! What a chapter to the illustrious record of this most favored town! It seems almost needless to recite it here, where every event was brought home to your own fireside, in the personal history of every father, and brother, and son who went forth to war; where the charities of the hour were dispensed with unbounded liberality; and where the bereavements of the conflict were brought home to many a sorrow-stricken heart. And yet an amazing chapter this is—casting into the shade the marvels of romance, and all the heroic adventure that poet ever painted.

A New England youth, with the blood of the
Puritan running in his veins, and the stern resolve
of the Puritan slumbering in his heart, had passed
his days in the quiet pleasures and pursuits of a
New England village. His mind had been cultivated in the simple and useful studies of the
district school. He had been taught to " forgive
his enemies," as the foundation of true Christian
courage, and as the first step pointed out by Him
who is the way, and the truth, and the life. He
had adopted the honest calling of his fathers,—
resolved to preserve those manly and reliable
qualities which had given his people their power
and influence through many generations. The
traditions of the old wars, and trials, and successes of his country, the trophies of his ancestors hanging on the walls of his humble dwell-
ing, taught him through what rugged paths his
rights and privileges as a citizen had come down
to him. When the nineteenth of April came
round, he had before him the bloody drama on
the village green of Lexington. When the seven-
teenth of June returned, he heard the roar of
the cannon on Bunker Hill, and saw "the thick
volumes of smoke and flame rising from the
burning Charlestown." He believed in the Republic, and in that portion of it especially known
as Massachusetts, the home of human equality,
of firm faith, and high aspiration. In the dim
and shadowy past stood the giant forms of the
mighty dead who had given his country power
and renown, types of heroic virtues in their
day and generation; watching with solemn and

earnest gaze from their celestial battlements, the country they had transmitted to their sons.

It is not easy to imagine the event which could burst upon this young man's home, and provide him with a new existence, in which all his slumbering energies might find inspiration. But the event came. The existence of that Union he had been taught to love, was threatened, and the echoes of the signal gun of rebellion, reverberating across the land, reached his quiet home. From that moment a life of heroism commenced. Obedient to the first call of his country, he received the blessing of his mother, turned away with hidden emotion from his sister's tears, summoned his manliness, and entered upon his career. The trials of the rendezvous, the jar and tumult of the multitude, the weary march, the loneliness and solitude of a life with an unknown crowd, the intense excitement of desperate adventure, and oh! that longing and aching thought of home! what a weight to bear, as he joined that first regiment from Massachusetts, and hastened to defend and save the capital from the tread of the invader. Amidst the hardships of the camp, the wildness of battle, the weariness of the march, the burning heat, and the biting cold, now stunned and blinded in the charge, and now a patient sufferer in the hospital, in prison to-day, and in the very jaws of death to-morrow, he performs the self-sacrificing duty which his country has imposed upon her defenders. The disasters of the Union army are his sorrows—its successes are his joys. He follows his flag in

c

victory and defeat—disheartened never—perhaps with Meade at Gettysburg, perhaps with Sheridan in the valley, perhaps with Hooker at Lookout Mountain, perhaps with Grant at Vicksburg, perhaps with Sherman at Atlanta, perhaps toiling in the wilderness, perhaps entering Richmond on that glorious morning when the loyal host passed through its gates, and planted the Flag of the Union on its rebellious ramparts; and oh, distressing chance of ruthless war! perhaps cut down on the very eve of victory, and borne hither to fill a grave around which the tenderest affections, and the most heroic memories now cluster.

Can you tell me where in song or story a life like this, with all its emotions, has been recorded? Around the memory of this youth, and thousands such as he, gather all the gentle associations which soften and beautify the savagery of war. History has immortalized the generous and self-sacrificing deed of Sir Philip Sidney, as he stayed the hand which would moisten his own parched and dying lip, until the agony of his expiring comrade had been relieved. Shall not history also tell of him, whose last words were " Write to mother and tell her I behaved well;" of him, whose glazed eye was turned upon the picture of his child so far away, held there in his stiffening grasp; of him, who defiant of wounds rushed on to battle still, and who fell at last with this message on his lips—" Tell my father I was dressing my line when I was hit;" of him, who clasped to his heart, in its last throb, the written words of her whom he loved; of him, who rejoiced in death, and only asked that he might be buried in his own native town; of him, who preferred death on the picket-line to a surrender; of the thousands, who, we are told, rose superior to the agony of the hospital, and declared, as the holy light irradiated their pale faces, that they could die without regret, for the great and sacred cause? Shall not all this be told as the heavenly voice, uttered by Christian heroes bearing to the battle-field all the moral obligations, and kind affections, and pious sentiment, and intelligent devotion of free and educated Christian homes?

Such was the American soldier in the great conflict for freedom; and such was the inspiration he received from his relations to a Christian people in whose cause he fought, and for whose faith he fell. And, then, what a radiant atmosphere of charity, and religion and humanity, was gathered about him, as he discharged his high service. The prayers which followed the Crusaders in their warlike march to the Holy Sepulchre, the stern religious faith which inspired the hosts of Cromwell, the fires of freedom which lighted the path of our armies in the Revolution, were all cold and dull when compared with that fervid devotion to liberty and humanity, which glowed in the hearts of the loyal American people during the great war. What unbounded charities were lavished on our soldiers! Tell me, if you can, the town in which societies were not organized for their relief. Tell me, if you can, the church in which prayers were not uttered in their behalf. Fingers that had previously known no toil, labored for them incessantly. Female devotion, in camp, in hospital, at home, became a national virtue. The fact that we had an army in such a field, seemed to warm the American heart to the most generous sentiments, and to fill the American mind with the loftiest thought. When Phelps and Fremont proclaimed freedom as the law for all territory occupied by their armies; when Andrew announced that for personal liberty the people of Massachusetts would never cease to fill the ranks; when Lincoln sent forth his Emancipation Proclamation, as the holiest object of the war; they uttered only the voice of the faithful, whose holy zeal had become the life-blood of the nation. This it was which silenced the unfriendly words of foreign powers, and won for our cause a popular response abroad which jealous potentates dared not defy. They indeed learned to respect our valor on the field. The work performed at Vicksburg, and Gettysburg, and Nashville, and Atlanta, taught them that Grant, and Sherman, and Meade, and Thomas, were generals upon whose military power the most warlike nation might rely. The guns of Farragut and Winslow proclaimed our supremacy on the high seas, over the watery grave of the Alabama, and the silenced forts of New Orleans and Mobile. But the all-conquering force—that which robbed the designs of Great Britain of all popular support at home,—that which threw disgrace around the efforts of Louis Napoleon to plant an ally to the rebellion on this continent—was the devotion of our people to the cause of freedom and universal human rights, during the war. All honor then to our armies! All honor to those who led us on to victory! But glory and honor and gratitude to those who clothed the war with the robes of charity—to those who elevated it to the most humane purpose—to those who amidst the smoke and carnage of battle, led the American people on to national purity and redemption. As we hallow the graves of the dead, and erect monumental structures to their memory, let us not forget their illustrious comrades in civil life, who sanctified the cause for which they fell. On a day like this we may invoke the spirits of Abraham Lincoln and John A. Andrew, to bless us in our work, as they once blessed these dead heroes in theirs. On a day like this we may pay a grateful tribute to the great charities of the war—and learn that in the exercise of heroic virtues there is no distinction of race or sex or condition among the children of God.

I congratulate this town upon the part it has performed once and again in the great drama of this age. It is the same story, I know, repeated so often, in the thousands of towns throughout the North—but none the less admirable and instructive. You, who sit here, have not forgotten the prompt and ready response to every call for men to fill up the ranks of our armies, decimated by disease and death. Year after year the call was made upon you, and year after year was the same response given. I learn from your faithful and accurate historian, that your bounties were offered freely and liberally; that your quota was more than filled; that you provided for the families of the soldiers absent; that you expended more than twenty-seven thousand dollars in the work; and that you sent two hundred and forty-four soldiers into the army, being nine more than the town's quota. The private bounty and charity of the town, moreover, were increasing. The sons and brothers who were in the field, were not forgotten by the mothers and sisters who remained behind. And we are truly told that "Lexington also furnished one hospital nurse, whose services were scarcely surpassed by any of that class of self-sacrificing women, who submitted to every hardship, and encountered every danger, to relieve the sufferings of the patriotic defenders of our free institutions;" one devoted and kind-hearted American woman, let me add, who, having dispensed her charity with a liberal hand during the struggles of her own country, has devoted herself also to alleviating the sufferings of the wounded and stricken on the battle-fields of Europe, brethren of him to whom she had given her heart, and whose spirit and memory attend her in her heavenly service.

There are those here who cannot forget that sad story that out of the number who went hence into battle, twenty laid down their lives in their country's service. On an occasion like this we are all reminded of their labors, their sufferings, their death. At their graves, as the annual pilgrimage comes round, we recall their lives, we remember their service, we renew our vows to our country, and we offer with grateful hands the fairest tribute which nature has provided as a crown to her favorite sons. While we sympathize with the domestic sorrow which is renewed every day in those sacred solitudes where their voices are no longer heard;—with her, whose daily walk is attended by the sainted form of that beloved son, now closer than ever to her heart, and crowned with perennial youth;—with her, whose sad pleasure it is to see each day in the faces of her children, the features of their father, and to hear his voice in theirs;—with him, who is hastening to join that son upon whom he hoped to lean in the evening walk of life:—we rejoice and thank God for the example of heroism and valor which they have bequeathed to us and our country as a rich inheritance. Strew, then, their graves with flowers. Embalm their memories in your hearts. May the sod which covers them be sacred forever. And as the winds pass over their graves, may they bear to the remotest regions of our land the sacred story of their lives, and the beauty and significance of their deaths. And when the last of their comrades shall have gone to his rest, and the Grand Army shall all be mustered in heaven, may each returning spring take up the hallowed duty, and crown these mounds, to teach coming generations the sweet harmony which exists between the bountiful heart of creation, and the life and death of her brave, and true-hearted, and devoted sons.

The erection of a monumental structure to the memory of your fallen heroes, as a sacred object upon which the eyes of your children and your children's children to the remotest generation may rest, is in obedience to that natural sentiment of gratitude, which has adorned the civilized world with enduring memorials of noble deeds and noble men. A Memorial Hall dedicated to such historic events as attend the name of Lexington, and adorned with appropriate statues and tablets, possesses an interest for the mind of every American citizen. To those generous benefactors, who have contributed so largely towards the erection and adornment of this structure, not this community alone, but the nation owes a debt of gratitude. And were the distinguished and accomplished first President of your Monument Association, the classic orator and statesman of the last generation in Massachusetts alive to-day, I am sure you would hear from his silver tongue an approving and encouraging word for a design which in combining historical emblems and records, with the culture of books, and accommodation for the exercise of the rights and privileges of independent citizens, represents the genius as well as the kindly affections of our people. It is not given to all to unite in one Memorial Hall, the memory of the soldiers of two great wars for progress and humanity. Nor did the distinguished and public-spirited benefactors who interested themselves to

perpetuate by enduring monument the heroic
deeds enacted here by the revolutionary fathers,
anticipate such a fortunate combination as this.
Now, indeed, may the humblest student sitting
within this sacred hall, remember that for the
freedom of thought which gives an inestimable
value to the volume in his hands, the youthful
blood of two generations of men in this town
has been freely shed. As he turns with pride to
the history of his country and learns there the
great virtues and the social and civil principles,
which make a people truly powerful, contem-
plating also with pride the statues of the illustrious men who practiced these virtues in the
beginning, and fixed these principles, he can turn
then to the tablets which adorn these walls, and
learn the price which you have paid for the
preservation of the blessed institutions transmitted to us by the fathers. I have stood
beneath the triumphal arches, which have told
for ages the story of ancient warriors, and have
sorrowfully studied on those tablets, the mournful
processions of drooping captives. I have paused
in the great halls designed for the repose of
veterans of the Grand Army of Napoleon, or
for the naval heroes of the mistress of the seas.
I have lingered in the shadow of the proud
column which records the imperial triumphs of
personal ambition; but in all the significance, in
all the associations, which give true value to the
memorial of great events, they were low and
mean, when compared with this structure, which
invites an intelligent people within its walls, and

D

perpetuates the memory of a war fought for freedom and the elevation of mankind. Let it be understood hereafter that the triumphs of the American sword mean the advancement of religion and education.

Turning now, my friends, from the glorious record of the past, and pausing reverently before the memorials of American heroism and devotion which you this day dedicate, let us consider, for a moment, what we have accomplished for ourselves and for mankind by our great wars. For ourselves, by the revolution, an independent nationality, built upon such foundations that a great civil convulsion was not only tolerable, but promotive of all the progressive design which lay close to the hearts of our fathers. The revolutionary war, small in all its proportions, secured to mankind the first opportunity for a free republic, as the result of natural development, and not of violence or convulsion. The great war for the Union not only confirmed our nationality, but revealed its true proportions, purified it, brought it back to the sublime object of its founders, taught the world to respect its skill and valor in conflict on land and on sea, and to admire its devotion to the broadest doctrines of human rights as the foundation of good government. Our first step won the admiration of the thoughtful—our last won the respect of the arrogant and the thoughtless. In less than a century we have risen from colonial feebleness, to a commanding national presence, an empire, the only one known in history which foreign foe

has never vanquished, and which a great civil
strife has merely purified and strengthened.
History records that each succeeding step in
the work has been honorable;—but of the last
great conflict, its magnitude and its results are
so amazing, that even now it seems to us as if it
must have been a dream. Covering an extent
of territory as broad as all Europe; calling into
the field larger bodies of armed men, than any
similar event of modern times; conducted upon
a scale of operations unknown before, and in
accordance with the breadth of our possessions,
and the activity and normal condition of our
citizen soldiery; complicated with difficult political questions at home, and still more difficult
problems abroad; it constitutes a chapter in
history upon which the student will always linger
with amazement and romantic interest. In the
sudden and rapid development of military genius;
in the organization of great armies; in the rapidity of evolution; in the extent of its operations;
in the improvement of all the enginery of war;
in the social revolution; and in the solution of
constitutiona' questions which had long existed
between the states and the general government;
—the work of a century was accomplished during the four years' conflict. Such a tremendous
struggle could not but result either in great good
or great evil. As the flood swept on, it became
manifest that it must act as an agent of destruc-
tion, unless it left in its path the fertilizing
deposit, as the bed of a new and more luxuriant
harvest. That it preserved the best government

ever instituted by man, would seem to be a sufficient answer to any candid mind, which would
fairly estimate its consequences. That it swept
away a great social wrong, and purged the Con-
stitution and the statute-book of all complicity
with that wrong, is a still more satisfactory
consideration. That this is the accepted faith of
the American people, I cannot for a moment
doubt. Looking back over the history of the
past, they have learned to respect the power of
our government, and to admire and adore its
spirit. The guardian now of every citizen, it
stretches forth its hands for the protection of all
against injustice and wrong under every form,
offering education in the one, and the ballot in
the other, as the sure foundations of social and
civil equality and freedom, and national prosperity and strength.

Fortunately for ourselves, and as I think for
the prospects of republican freedom everywhere,
we stand no longer as a rival or a dependent
among the nations of the earth, but as an ally
and equal for all who are advancing towards free
institutions; as a rebuke to despotism everywhere. Recognizing the necessity and the destiny, that our institutions must one day cover
this entire continent, not by conquest, but by the
peaceful adoption of free and aspiring people;
remembering that "the Continental Congress,
by solemn resolution invited Canada, and then
appointed a commission with Benjamin Franklin
at its head, to form a union between the colonies and the people of Canada;" remembering

too the expression of Congress to these people, "that their interests and ours are inseparably united;" remembering, also, the written declaration of Richard Cobden to Charles Sumner more than twenty years ago, that "nature has decided that Canada and the United States must become one for all purposes of inter-communication;" and remembering, moreover, the broad and statesmanlike assertion of Mr. Sumner that, "the United States can never be indifferent to Canada, nor to the other British provinces, near neighbors and kindred;" I anticipate the time when the American flag shall protect the American citizen, on all lands and seas, from the Frozen ocean to the Isthmus, as a reward for that manly assertion and endeavor, which have taught foreign powers the strength of republican institutions to preserve themselves from overthrow, and to exercise an imperial sway, when necessary, without the exercise of despotic powers. We are now wise enough to "ask for nothing but what is right;" and we are powerful enough "to submit to nothing which is wrong." Composed of all nationalities, we would sympathize with all in their endeavors after freedom and education. To a united German Republic, advancing we trust to her place among the nations, we extend a cordial hand. To convulsed, and bleeding, and betrayed France, we present the calm power of our own republic, and the "moderation and wisdom that tempered our Revolution," in which her own great son learned his first lesson, and performed his first noble service. For Ireland we offer our fervent prayers;—and to England we extend our warning voice, that she may learn justice and honor ere it is too late.

Our revolutionary fathers heard in the British Parliament the appeals of Edmund Burke for conciliation and peace with the colonies; they listened to the thunders of Chatham when he rejoiced " that America had resisted; " they were cheered by the burning words of Barrè as he protested against the oppressive acts of the ministry towards their brethren in America. We do not forget the fountains of our republican thought— the genius of Milton, the doctrines of the Puritans, the assertions of Magna Charta. We speak the language of Shakspeare, and Milton, and Bacon, and Newton. We study with reverent interest that scene of the Pilgrim embarkation in the Rotunda of the American Capitol; and we pass beneath the same scene in the corridors of the Parliament House in England, the most conspicuous of all the national frescoes there.

We have not yet forgotten, I trust, the warm assurances of sympathy, during our civil war, from John Bright, and Thomas Hughes, and Newman Hall. We know well that the liberal heart of England and the freedom-loving heart of America beat in unison. But we cannot shut our eyes to the other side—that side full of insult and wrong, in which England from the days of the Boston Port Bill, down to the ravages of the Alabama has always been the aggressor. The flings of her statesmen against what they have seen fit to call " an unbalanced democracy " here;

the contempt of her scholars for American thought, until Hawthorne, and Longfellow and Emerson conquered their prejudices; her aggressive acts towards our commerce and our fisheries; her swift recognition of rebel belligerency; her chronic antagonisms to American nationality,— have inflicted a wound on the national heart not easily healed. But now let the quarrels between the mother and the daughter cease; and let them join in one great civilizing mission. While the United States have earned the power to call for instant redress for wrongs inflicted upon themselves, they have also earned the right to protest against acts of injustice towards others, and to encourage all the popular aspirations which have been excited by the success of their own free institutions.

Will not England learn her lesson, the lesson taught her by her child, whom she sent forth from her home, two centuries and a half ago? Can she resist forever the demands for free education, the ballot, equal inheritance, and division of land? Will nothing but impending ruin induce her to lift her heavy hand from Ireland, and allow her people to rise to the full stature of elevated and prosperous humanity? Will she never learn that the example set by a young, free, busy, prosperous and powerful nation is worth studying, and that a peaceful alliance with a republic holding in its hands the great highway from ocean to ocean, possesses commercial advantages, which are as valuable at

least as uneasy and unproductive colonial possessions?

From the 19th of April, 1775, to the 19th
of April, 1871, the great American Republic
has been advancing " from strength to strength,"
working out the problem submitted to her, when
she entered the family of nations. From first to
last, what has she not done to awaken popular
thought, to instruct the wise, to inspire the
brave? The inevitable centre, hereafter, of the
great commercial enterprises of the world, it is
her system of government, her form of civilization, and, I trust, her national honor and honesty,
which are to be an example for all men. And
when the two nations which separated on that
" glorious morning," on the green of Lexington,
shall join hands again, the signal will be given
for international honor, and peace, and arbitra-
tion, and justice, to take the place of jealousy,
and wrong, and injustice, and confusion, and
war. The lesson, which, in all our strange experiences and vicissitudes, we have taught ourselves
and others, may never be forgotten. And with
hearts filled with gratitude to God, who hath
given us the victory, and so protected our
country that we can proudly call around us the
heroic memories of two great wars, on this
historic day, may we renew our vows to be true
to our great inheritance, and to transmit it in all
its glory to our children, for the beauty of the
whole earth.

PROCEEDINGS

AT THE

Dedication of the Town and Memorial Hall,

LEXINGTON, MASS.

APRIL 19, 1871.

At the annual town meeting held in March, 1871, the Building Committee of the New Town Memorial and Library Halls Building reported the work nearly completed and ready for delivery to the town. It was voted that the Building be dedicated with appropriate ceremonies on the 19th of April, being the ninety-sixth anniversary of the battle of Lexington, and a committee of eight citizens, to be joined to the members of the Building Committee, were constituted a Committee of Arrangements with discretionary powers to carry out the vote, and an appropriation of a sum not exceeding three hundred dollars was made. The Committee of Arrangements was organized with the following gentlemen as members thereof, viz:—

Of the Building Committee:—Messrs. Charles Hudson, John Hastings, Sargent C. Whicher, Hammon Reed, Luke C. Childs, Warren E. Russell, and Reuben W. Reed.

Of other citizens joined:—Messrs. George W. Robinson, Joseph N. Brewer, George Munroe, Matthew H.

Merriam, Oliver P. Mills, Alonzo Goddard, Charles E. Goodwin, and Charles Blodgett; to whom the following gentlemen were added by the Committee, namely :—Loring W. Muzzey, Charles M. Parker, George L. Stratton, George E. Muzzey, and Frederic Witherell.

At the same meeting it was considered appropriate that the formalities of receiving the keys from the Building Committee, should be tendered the young men of the town, as significant of the prospective provision, kept prominently in view in the design and erection of the building, for the wants and privileges of those who are to come after and succeed the passing generation.

In accordance with this spirit, Messrs. James E. Parker, Billings Smith, jr., Eugene Tuttle, and Charles S. Blodgett, were appointed a Representative Committee to receive the keys, as the emblems of the trust confided to them.

An enthusiastic interest prevailed in the community for the creditable success of the contemplated ceremonies, enhanced by a spirit of patriotism and grateful remembrance of sacrifices in war, which were on this occasion to be formally expressed in the consecration of the Memorial Hall. Citizens responded liberally by placing at the disposal of the Committee necessary funds for the execution of their plans.

The morning of the 19th of April dawned auspiciously. The Hall, the old Monument, and many private residences, were gaily decked with the national colors, appropriate mottoes and emblems. The inauguration of the festivities of the day was announced by a salute of artillery at sunrise, which was repeated at noon and at sunset. At eleven o'clock the procession was formed on the ground in front of the railroad depot, in the following order :—

Germania Band, 20 pieces, conducted by A. Heinicke.
Col. John W. Hudson, Chief Marshal.
Assistant Marshal, Lieut. Jarvis W. Dean.
Detachment of Malden Battery, Lieut. W. B. Patterson,
Commanding.
Hancock Engine Company.
Assistant Marshal, Lieut. George E. Muzzey.
Public Schools of the Town, about two hundred children in all.
Assistant Marshal, Lieut. Samuel E. Chandler.
Committee of Arrangements and Building Committee.
Committee of Young Men.
President of the Day, Orator and Chaplain.
Distinguished Civilians.
Clergymen of Lexington.
Other Civic Guests.
Assistant Marshal, Major Jonas F. Capelle.
Officers of the United States Army
Lieut. Col. John G. Chandler and Capt. Lewis E. Crone.
Soldiers of the War of 1812.
Officers and Soldiers of the last War, from Lexington, together
with those from other places, now resident in the Town.
Assistant Marshal, Capt. William Plummer.
Town Officers.
Citizens generally.

The route of the procession was from the place of forming, up Main and Monument streets, around the Common, and thence to the Hall.

After a voluntary by the band the Chief Marshal introduced ASA COTTRELL, Esq., President of the day, who on assuming the duties of the place, addressed the audience as follows :

ADDRESS OF ASA COTTRELL, ESQ.

" *Ladies and Gentlemen* :

" The returning year has again brought around the vernal season, and the day on which, ninety-six years ago, the brave men whose lineal descendants are among those here present, stood and offered the first resistance to the scarlet-coated soldiery of Britain, on the soil of this very town, then bearing the same name which it bears now, and that name was rendered, then and there, by their deeds, historical and immortal.

" Yes, that name LEXINGTON stirs the spirit of every true American as the sound of a trumpet ; it is associated forever with the early history of the heroic age of that people, who now stand foremost in the march of empire, of freedom, of civilization, and of progress. And here on this peaceful day, in this peaceful time, having recently passed through the great crisis which so long threatened to blast the hopes of our ancestors, and of good men everywhere, we, citizens of Lexington and of the United States, no longer drenched in fraternal blood, and far from the din of carnage and sights of horror, whose echo and whose shadow beyond the broad ocean contrast with our own sense of preservation, and solid ground of security and rejoicing ; we, hopeful, and with reason, of our country's glory and its future, are to-day gathered.

" We are assembled here for a happy cause and for a worthy purpose. An event, slight perhaps in itself, slight by comparison with the fall of empires, or the conquests of kings ; but yet pleasant as a symbol of peace and the success of democratic government, has summoned and collected us here. That event is the completion of this Hall. It is a mark of the growth of the town, and an important epoch in its history. It is a sign that a republican system of government, by the people for themselves, is not falling into disrepute or deterioration.

"We are here to honor the occasion with some fitting ceremonial. We are here in the presence of each other, our townsmen, their wives, their families and friends collectively, to look with our own eyes on this proof of progress and advance.

"The town hall, the church and the school-house, are to be seen and have long been visible, on every hill, and in every valley in New England. These, far more than the lines of railway and their station-houses and depots: more even than the wonderful wire-work over which the lightning, as man's slave, bears the latest intelligence of all that has most recently passed on this planet: far more even than the thriving farm and substantial farm-house, or the ornamental villa: far more than the myriad manufactories, many windowed and storied: far more than the crowded and lofty warehouses of yonder city, each one of which is a princely fortune: far more than the thick clustering masts of the shipping about its wharves: far more than our universities, our parks, our opera houses, our hotels: more than all these, the village town-house, now massive and substantial: the airy school-house, not devoid of architectural pretensions, that has taken the place of the primitive single-roomed log-cabin in the midst of the forest: and the heaven-pointing spires in every hamlet and borough, indicate the spirit of our age and nation: these are the true exponents of the character and intelligence of our people: these are the jewels of our country: these show our manner of living and our life: these tell to all, the way in which the descendants of the pilgrims aim to secure and enjoy the highest possible blessings of human existence—liberty, knowledge, and virtue.

"Here shall the men, and perhaps the women, come to determine what shall be the laws, and who shall make and administer them, with the power to change both the laws and the law ministers, at their own sovereign will and pleasure. The state-house, and the court-house and the prison, have no terrors to us, while we contemplate this structure—for if oppression and injustice emanate from or await us there—here we will come and within these walls, by our votes, abolish or change them.

"These new and numerous, and fair but not magnificent or extravagant edifices, are the best sign of the general welfare. Gorgeous cathedrals, royal palaces and massive pyramids, conjure up memories of the munificence of despotism ; but wide-spread and universal comfort, and not isolated grandeur, is the harvest we and our fathers have sowed and cultivate. The monuments of our national glory, are our improvements in every thing that increases the intelligence and happiness of the general people, diminishes pain and suffering, elevates the dignity of man, and enlarges enlightened and safe freedom for the whole. And therefore, with devout and grateful hearts, we are assembled to receive this Building from those intrusted with the task of erecting and completing it, and to render our acknowledgments for the zeal, energy and fidelity with which their commission has been executed.

"As on yonder Common, stands the Monument of Lexington's early heroes, here to-day, we hail the emblem of the true meaning and value of their immortal labors. Here, when the citizens shall from time to time meet together, these tablets, trophies, statues and mementoes, and the associations clustering about them, will renew their patriotism, and increase their love of country. If civil discord has so recently nearly shattered the edifice of our national greatness and safety, never may this Hall, while that memory lasts, jar with selfish and sectional hate and strife. Here let local and partizan jealousy have no room ; let the genius of the place prohibit it ; let the name of Lexington be associated with Concord.

"This Building owes its erection in part, as you know, to private and patriotic bounty, which demands, and will never fail to receive with us, due acknowledgment, and the best meed of being understood and appreciated. This Hall is not only for us, but for those who are to come after us, and fill the places that we now fill. To the young men of this town, this noble edifice is to be this day committed. They are to maintain it in the future, and hence they formally receive it, and become its sponsors. Let them, then, regard it as a sacred legacy, and honor it as such, cherishing the suggestions and monitions of the wise and eloquent men who are present to address them, for to them we look, to perpetuate all those glorious associations that now cluster around and hallow it.

" *Ladies and Gentlemen :*

"This Hall having been completed to the acceptance of the gentlemen who were appointed to superintend its erection, it remains for them to submit to their constituents the result of their labors, and formally vest it in the authorities of the town. The Committee now desire to attend to that duty by their chairman.

" Let me invite your attention to a gentleman, who, for a score of his best years, with great ability and zeal, has devoted himself to your progress and material advancement. Any words of commendation I might attempt to offer, would fall so far short of the meed of praise your own thoughts would suggest, that they would rather detract from than add to his conceded merits.

" Allow me to introduce to you the Hon. CHARLES HUDSON, Chairman of the Building Committee."

Mr. HUDSON, in behalf of the Building Committee, tendered the keys to the Committee of Young Men, with the following address :

ADDRESS OF HON. CHARLES HUDSON.

" *Mr. Chairman :*

"The committee intrusted with the important duty of erecting a public edifice to meet the wants of the town, present and prospective, congratulate you and themselves that the object of their appointment is so far accomplished that they can with propriety submit their work to their constituents, and respectfully ask to be discharged from any further substantive labor on the subject.

"The committee, from their first appointment, have felt that they assumed a high responsibility in urging their fellow citizens to embark in an enterprise which would impose upon the town a heavy pecuniary burden ; and though we were aware of the wants of the place, we should have deemed it prudent to defer action on the subject till the town had reduced its outstanding debt ; but for the liberal offer of a native of Lexington, a worthy and patriotic lady of whom we may justly be proud. Mrs. MARIA CARY, of Brooklyn, N. Y., moved by a generous regard for the place of her nativity, offered to the town six thousand dollars on condition that we should erect an edifice which would meet the wants of the public, and at the same time furnish a Memorial Hall in honor of our departed patriots, and a suitable room for the Free Library, which she had partially endowed. And though at the time of our meeting, when the vote to build was taken, she was traveling in a foreign land, we were persuaded that distance would not alienate nor the wide Atlantic quench her regard for her native town : and that a manly effort and a generous trust on our part, would secure to us further aid. And in this we were not disappointed. For our generous benefactress has enlarged her donation to twenty thousand dollars—four thousand for the Memorial Hall, six thousand for the Library, and ten thousand for the edifice itself. With these benefactions for such worthy objects, the town of Lexington can well afford to contract a debt.

" In the construction of the Building we have endeavored to meet the present and future wants of the town, rather than to provide rooms to rent. The general design of the committee, modified and molded by the skill and taste of the architect, has been adopted ; and the execution of the plan carried out by the art and the untiring fidelity of the contractors has given us an edifice of which we may justly be proud. The division we have made of the interior may require a brief explanation. We have sometimes been told that our Library Hall was too large. But we have fondly looked forward to a time when not only the increase of books will require more room, but when the wants of the people will demand a reading room, and their taste a cabinet of historic relics, and a collection of specimens illustrative of the arts and sciences, and when the walls may be adorned with portraits and paintings.

" Our Memorial Hall requires a passing notice. Though its conception is original, we are not ashamed of its design. It is consecrated to the memory of the departed, and its emblems illustrate their patriotism, and show our gratitude. Our statues, we regret to say, are not completed, but will be in a few months. As you approach the Memorial Hall from the front entrance, you will, when these statues are in position, see in the niche nearly in front of you on the left, a life-sized marble statue of a soldier of 1775—a minuteman, leaving his plough and seizing his musket and powder-horn at the call of his country, and with a countenance which bespeaks firmness of purpose and trust in the Lord of Hosts, standing forth to resist aggression, and, if need be, sacrifice his life in the cause of freedom. On his right is a marble tablet, bearing the names of the gallant men of Lexington who fell on the memorable 19th of April, 1775, fulfilling the pledge previously given, that they would be faithful unto death.

" In the niche, nearly in front of you on the right, stands a marble statue, representing the class of men who rallied

F

under the flag of the Union, when treason raised its impious hand against our country; and on his left you can read the names of the devoted men of the Lexington quota, who perished in defence of our liberties. We recognize them as our late neighbors, friends, and protectors, apparently retiring from the field after they had performed their whole duty. They seem to us a reserved corps of freedom's ardent votaries, watchfully reposing upon their arms to guard the interests of the Republic. We are awed in their presence; and with grateful emotion silently breathe forth the benediction :—

> " ' Rest, patriot soldiers ! be your names revered ;
> Your valor shielded what our fathers reared.'

" But facing these statues are two empty niches, anxiously waiting to be filled by the statues of two illustrious men of the Revolution, endeared to the whole country, and particularly identified with Lexington, and the day we celebrate. When one of these niches is filled with a statue of the first signer of the Declaration of Independence, whose name on that immortal instrument stands out in bold relief, showing at once his patriotism and his penmanship ; and the other is filled with that of the sturdy patriot who organized the American Revolution, and who, when he heard the report of the British guns on Lexington Common on the 19th of April, '75, exclaimed in prophetic rapture, ' What a glorious morning for America is this !' then we shall have a Memorial Hall worthy of the birth-place of American liberty, and shall have done something to perpetuate the memory of John Hancock and Samuel Adams, two of

> " ' The few immortal names
> That were not born to die.'

" And these niches must be filled. The friends of these distinguished statesmen and patriots ask it ; the public voice demands that it be done. Thus far we have been mostly dependent upon female generosity. Not only Mrs. CARY, but Mrs. SAMUEL B. RINDGE, of Cambridge, a native of Lexington, has substantially erected one of our statues, and Mrs. EBENEZER SUTTON, of Peabody, has made us a liberal gift toward filling the vacant niches. Such examples should excite the gentlemen to action, and so furnish us with the needed funds.

"Mr. Chairman, we have already said that, in erecting this edifice, we have looked forward to the future growth of the town. We have built it not so much for ourselves as for those that come after us—for our children and our children's children. Impressed with this view, the town has done well in selecting a committee of young men to receive the hall in her name. You, young gentlemen, have been made the honored agents to represent not only the Lexington of to-day, but the Lexington that is to be. You stand as an intermediate link between us and posterity. It is with peculiar pleasure, therefore, that we pass this Building over to you, who, according to the course of nature, will enjoy it when we shall have passed off the stage. Here you will assemble for the transaction of public business. In this Hall you will convene to hear public lectures, to interchange kind offices, to join in social gatherings, and to partake of such innocent amusements as are calculated to dispel gloom, and give that variety which has been denominated the spice of life. But you must remember that this Hall is not the entire building, nor is this edifice the only thing committed to your care. There are institutions connected with it, more valuable than the brick and mortar of which its walls are composed. The Memorial Hall embodies the spirit of patriotism which made, and still preserves us a free people; and the Library Hall is but the portal to that field of knowledge on which personal enjoyment and public prosperity must depend. These institutions you will fondly cherish. To you, young men, we look with confidence, that you will exert your influence

to fill the niches in the one hall, and the shelves in the
other, so that patriotism may be chastened with knowledge,
and that both may combine to make us an enlightened,
free and prosperous community. But the time-piece behind
me, that faithful monitor, the gift of one of our prominent
citizens,* admonishes me to draw my remarks to a close.
I bow to the admonition, and will deliver to you these keys
as emblematic of this edifice and the institutions it embo-
soms, with an ardent hope and a firm belief that these
great interests will be cherished, and that what is committed
to you will be handed down unimpaired to those that shall
come after you."

Mr. JAMES E. PARKER, in behalf of the Committee of
Young Men, responded as follows :

ADDRESS OF JAMES E. PARKER, ESQ.

" *Mr. Chairman :—*
" On behalf of the town of Lexington, more particularly
the young men of the town, whom I have the honor to
represent, I receive these keys from your hands, believing
that the mechanical execution of the work has been thorough and complete, and that great credit is due the contractors for the faithful discharge of their duties. It also
becomes my pleasant duty to express to you, sir, personally,
and to your colleagues on the Building Committee, the
sense of obligation which the people of the town feel
toward you for the untiring exertions which you have made
that this structure might be what it is, a credit to the town,
and perhaps no unworthy memorial of those brave men
who struggled not far from here, ninety-six years ago to-
day, and of those equally brave men who, later, (in the
language of the lamented Lincoln,) gave up their lives that
the nation might live, and whose bones, in many instances,

* GEORGE W. ROBINSON, Esq.

still rest in that 'sacred' Southern soil, sacred indeed, now that they have consecrated it with their blood."

The dedicatory prayer was then offered by Rev. A. B. Muzzey, Chaplain of the day. After which the President of the day introduced Dr. George B. Loring, who delivered the eloquent oration which has been kindly furnished us for publication.

At the close of the oration, after music by the band, the following original hymn, composed for this occasion by Mrs. C. A. Means, was sung by the assembly.

> Our fathers, true and brave,
> Here gave their lives, to save
> Our land so dear:
> God, whom they loved, their shield;
> Their watch-word, "Die, not yield,"
> On many a well fought field,
> They knew no fear.

> Once more at Freedom's call,
> Sons left their homes to fall,
> No more to rise:
> Worthy their fathers' fame,
> We hold each honored name,
> And praise with loud acclaim
> And tear-dimmed eyes.

> Thank God, the strife is o'er;
> Peace crowns our land once more
> With heavenly light;
> These walls shall proudly tell
> How those we loved so well,
> For their dear country fell
> In deadly fight.

Long may the arts of peace
Bid strife and tumult cease,
  'Neath Learning's sway ;
While wisdom rules our land,
Firm as a rock we'll stand,
Held by that mighty Hand
  Which guards our way.

This closed the exercises at the Hall, and the company proceeded to the Railroad depot, which had been tastily fitted up for the dinner. The tables were bountifully supplied, and were served to about four hundred persons.

The Divine blessing was invoked by the Rev. Chaplain.

After dinner, the President began the intellectual feast in saying :

" *Ladies and Gentlemen :*

" I feel that I should leave an important duty unfulfilled, if I did not, before vacating this chair, in behalf of the Committee of Arrangements and the citizens of this town generally, say a word of welcome to the gallant men who to-day represent the defenders of our most cherished rights.

" Just ten years ago to-day, some of you, whom I now have the honor to address, were marching to the defence of our common country. Just ten years ago, Massachusetts' good Governor, the ever blessed ANDREW, sent forth upon the wings of the lightning, to the yeomanry of old Middlesex, that the nation's capital was in danger, and the nation's life threatened : when, as the wand of the magician brings forth from hidden springs the wonders of his art, up sprang the men of Middlesex, ready to maintain the right, and strike the first blow to protect the liberties their fathers struck the first blow to secure. Worthy sons of heroic sires, welcome, thrice welcome, to this our festive gathering.

"And I am sure I could not render a more acceptable service to my fellow citizens assembled to-day, than to return their acknowledgments to the distinguished guests who have honored the occasion by their presence, and especially their thanks to the distinguished orator, whose unrivalled wisdom and eloquence have so instructed and charmed us.

"The happy events of this day will be long cherished by our citizens; esteeming it, however, but an interlude or introduction to the sublime spectacle, of the nation worshiping at the shrine of liberty on the 19th of April, 1875—believing that the nation's best and noblest men will make a pilgrimage to that spot, which was a field of blood in 1775, but which, in 1875, shall be a field of glory.

"And now permit me to introduce, as the toast-master for the occasion, a gentleman whom Lexington loves to honor—born amid the rugged hills of New England, a soldier on the plains of Mexico, a citizen true and loyal on the patriotic soil of Lexington—though absent from us for a season, we shall presently see that his absence has not diminished his patriotism, or abated his zeal in advocating universal freedom—I have the honor to introduce to you Colonel ISAAC H. WRIGHT.

Colonel WRIGHT proceeded to the duties assigned him in these words of welcome and congratulation.

ADDRESS OF COLONEL ISAAC H. WRIGHT.

" *Ladies and Gentlemen :*

"With little or no time for reflection and preparation, I have again revisited your ancient town upon the call of your Committee of Arrangements, to officiate as Toast-

Master at this most interesting festival. In default of time for pre-arranged and digested thought, I must trust to the inspiration of the occasion, and to your generous indulgence, for whatever of acceptance my impromptu labors may meet with at your hands.

"The President of the Day has imposed a heavy weight of obligation upon me, by the very complimentary terms in which he has presented me to this company, and in fact has left me but one course to pursue, in the absence of all hope on my part to realize the very exalted anticipations which his words would excite. And that course is, to put in a disclaimer, which I now do, against all and singular, the commendations with which he has so lavishly invested me. There being then a tacit convention that my friend Cottrell's high-wrought eulogium shall not be brought up in judgment against my short-comings, I may be permitted to say that whatever of justice and truth there may be in his remarks is properly attributable, in part at least, to circumstances which transpired in former days while I was a resident of Lexington.

"It will be remembered by many who now hear me, that many years ago, when that distinguished apostle of universal liberty, LOUIS KOSSUTH, made a pilgrimage to this town to do reverence at the shrine of the Massachusetts martyrs to American liberty, I had the honor to receive and introduce to the citizens of Lexington, that eminent scholar and enlightened patriot, from whose eloquent lips we heard with delight the avowal of those doctrines of universal political freedom, of which he was at once the exponent and the martyr. Upon that occasion and some others of a kindred public character, I had the pleasure, while a citizen of the town, of being identified in some humble capacity with the patriotic demonstrations of the people ; and I am willing to attribute to a grateful appreciation of my labors in that behalf, any small share of the commendations of your President which I may justly appropriate to myself.

"Lexington has done much in the past by her influence and example, to establish and uphold the cause of liberty and humanity. When, on the 19th of April, 1775, she was called upon to offer up her sons as a barrier to stay the triumphal march of the invading host, by that distinguished destiny a seal was set upon her brow: she was consecrated to Freedom's holy cause by a baptism of blood, and from that day forth a high and solemn mission devolved upon her. And well has she fulfilled that mission! Faithfully by her public schools, and her town-meetings—those infant schools of Republics—has she inculcated and cherished that enlightened and discriminating love of liberty, upon which the experiment of popular self-government was successfully founded in this country, almost a century ago. Freely has she sent forth her sons to do battle for the country on every field and on every ocean where the old Pine-Tree flag or the Stars and Stripes have heralded the battle for liberty or constitutional law. Generously has she poured forth her means to succor and sustain the wounded, and the widows and orphans of the honored dead. To-day, on this proud anniversary, her sons and daughters gather together in magnificent array to dedicate a noble Memorial Hall: a monument of patriotism replete with beauty, and crowned with usefulness.

"The past, then, at least is secure; the people of Lexington have thus far faithfully cherished her ancient fame, and kept alive within her bounds the fires of liberty. Nor do I doubt that in the time to come, the sons and daughters of this time-honored town will emulate the noble example of those who have gone before them, and by their patriotism and public spirit in all emergencies, whether of war or peace, fully meet the high expectations founded on a past so glorious. When I look around upon the earnest and intelligent faces that grace this festive board; when I consider the patriotic character of the large assembly which has this day crowded yonder beautiful Memorial Hall, and the deep and earnest attention with which the orator's eloquent and fitting address was listened to by all; I see an ample guarantee that Lexington will ever be true to her ancient fame, and that her sons and daughters will never fail to emulate the virtues of their predecessors.

"Let me now bespeak your attention to the Regular Toasts, as I shall announce them, and to the responses of the eloquent gentlemen whom I shall call upon to answer thereto."

First regular toast:

The President of the United States.

Response by the Band, "Hail Columbia," and cheers for the President.

Second regular toast:

The Governor of the Commonwealth—Illustrious in an illustrious line of succession of leaders that have steadily marshalled the State in the foremost rank.

Response by General S. E. CHAMBERLAIN of the Governor's staff, who gave some interesting reminiscences of the sons of Lexington in the late war.

Third regular toast:

The Army and Navy—Their recent exploits in war, by sea and land, demonstrate that the fathers inspired the sons and prompted them to noble deeds and heroic suffering.

Response by the Band, " Star Spangled Banner."

Fourth regular toast:

The Nation in 1783—*in* 1871—The infant Hercules in the cradle, and the resistless champion of right and justice.

Ex-Governor WALTER HARRIMAN, of New Hampshire, responded as follows:

In the brief moment allotted to me, of course, I can do no more than barely to *glance* at a theme like this :—The infant Hercules in the cradle, and the resistless champion of right and justice! What emotions this sentiment awakens! What patriotic fervor it inspires ! What national grandeur it brings to the foreground !

Look at our country to-day. What variety of soil, of climate, of production. Material riches are poured, with unstinted prodigality, at our feet. The " horn of plenty" is no fable. Everywhere we find the full stream of its bounty. And all this is free to our hand. No Chinese wall invests this country. It opens its doors wide to the down-trodden and the oppressed, and its invitation has the endorsement of its visible progress. What nation has enlarged its census roll, or its territorial area, or the individual prosperity of its citizens as ours has done ? Only two hundred and fifty years ago the Pilgrim Fathers stood on Plymouth Rock :

> Amid the storm they sang,
>   And the stars heard, and the sea ;
> And the sounding aisles of the dim woods rang
>   To the anthem of the free.

Before them, stretching from ocean to ocean, were the tangled wastes of a wilderness—the abiding-place of savage beasts and savage men. See, now, what marvellous contrast is presented. Look on the smiling face of the land. See the harvests of the West, and the white-winged commerce of the East ; how cities, towns, villages, have sprung up as if by the magic spell of enchantment ; how canals float our ships from lake to sea ; how railroads have laid their iron tramways over plains—spanning rivers—tunnelling mountains. See the churches whose spires lift the finger of prayer up into the sky : and the school-houses, which are the nurseries of American thrift, culture and statesmanship. All this, and more,—*aye, more !* the result of only ninety years of a government hardly equalled, certainly never excelled.

> O, Beautiful ! My Country ! ours once more !
>   What were our lives without thee ;
>   What *all our lives* to save thee ;
>   We reck not what we gave thee ;
>   We will not dare to doubt thee.
> Bow down, dear Land, for thou hast found release ;
>   Bow down, in prayer and praise ;
>   Thy God, in these distempered days,
> Hath taught thee the sure wisdom of His ways,
> And *through thine enemies* hath wrought thy peace.

Let the American citizen study the institutions fostered by this government; let him appreciate the freedom of the people; let him reverence, as he ought, the glory of our flag, which has caught within its folds a full constellation of stars, and then he will understand, in some measure, the significance of those talismanic words which are a passport and protection in every quarter of the globe—"*I am an American citizen!*"

Look over this country. No nation ever had so valuable territorial resources; none ever had given in trust such noble principles of government. The simple statement of a few facts is overwhelming. We have a frontier line of more than ten thousand miles. We have a sea-coast of four thousand, and a lake-coast of twelve hundred. The longest river in Europe— the famous Danube, which washes the feet of Vienna, is but half the size of our Mississippi. The song of the Rhine has been sung by every tongue, but even our *Ohio* is six hundred miles longer than that. The Thames flows by the Roman embankments which gave foothold to the city of London, but our little *Hudson* bears its wealth of merchandise and beauty to the bosom of New York, and is a hundred and twenty miles longer than the famous English stream. The whole of England might be put into the old State of Virginia, and yet leave margin enough to form a State nearly the size of Massachusetts! Our *territories* embrace over a billion of acres, with only a population of less than half a million. There is elbow-room for multitudes of people yet to come. A grand, prosperous, free home opens its doors with a wide hospitality in this country, to the deserving of all climes. And not only is there *land*, but there are the honest thrift and the resolute activity resulting from these great and generous national principles, which, like granite blocks cut from the quarry of eternity, underlie our governmental institutions. While, tried by fire, we have that last, that grandest of all possessions,—a clear, heroic, American *manhood*. This is the jewel in our crown: this, the central luminary in our constellation; this, the rich product of our fathers' fidelity; this, the chiefest boon to be transmitted to posterity.

Fifth regular toast:

Lexington Common and Concord North Bridge.

Response by Hon. J. M. Usher, who spoke of the glory of the early history of Lexington, and believed that the services of the day were a pledge that the future of the town would be equal to her past.

Sixth regular toast:

The Orator of the Day—The thrilling eloquence of his address is equalled only by his ardent patriotism.

Dr. George B. Loring responded:

I know of no position more difficult and embarrassing than that of the Orator of the Day, when called upon to respond to a toast complimentary to himself. Every other man in the community finds some one ready and willing to respond for him. Every topic finds an advocate. The Governor has his aide, who can present his case gracefully and eloquently. The President of the United States always has an admiring friend, who is ready to speak for him. The Flag has its eulogist; the "day we celebrate," its historian. But the unhappy orator is compelled, after having worn out the patience of the audience in one place, to test his powers on his own behalf, in another. And after my long and severe demand upon your time, I really feel ashamed to proceed again.

I must apologize for the length of my oration. It was a wise thought of my friend Mr. Hudson, when he urged brevity with his invitation. But I could not help it. The charm of the subject led me on; and I beg you and him to forgive me, and to charge upon yourselves the fault of having a fascinating history which led me away. And then there were certain associations, which I could not forget as the task went on. I remembered that to Essex County belongs a share of the glories of this early era and of this day. It was the courage and resolution of Col. Pickering and his little band, at the North Bridge in Salem which set an example not forgotten by the men of Lexington and Concord. It was John Felt, walking by the side of Col. Leslie on his march through Salem in search of secreted cannon, and threatening him with instant death if he ordered his men to fire, whose spirit attended me as I warmed my heart over the valor of your town. And the men

of Danvers, who rushed to the fray, leaving their comrades on
the field, the first offering of that patriotic town to the cause of
freedom; they too attended me in my labors. So too Abed-
nego Judkins of Swampscott, (I think that was the Puritanic
name he bore,) seizing his fowling-piece, and hastening to the
fight with unshod feet, and his half-cooked hoe-cake under his
arm, came on in the procession of Essex boys, to assure me that
of whatever I said for Middlesex, they would claim a share.
Do you wonder then that my story was a long one? To me I
assure you it is most interesting, and I thank most deeply your
Committee for giving me an opportunity to dwell for a season
among scenes and memories so grand. I give you—

The Revolutionary Heroes of Essex and Middlesex—Their
united devotion to the great cause of Freedom has never been
forgotten by their sons.

Seventh regular toast:

The Men of Lexington who fell on the 19th of April, 1775—
Good seed well sown; it has produced a harvest of glory.

Response by Rev. A. B. MUZZEY, a descendant of one
of the soldiers in the battle of Lexington:

Mr. President:

With the first knowledge of your intention to dedicate this
fair and substantial edifice on the 19th of April, I resolved to be
present as a spectator on the occasion. My attachment to my
native town grows more and more strong as I descend the vale
of years; and the connection of my own relatives with the
scenes of this ever-memorable day, increases and intensifies this
interest. One of the proto-martyrs, whose names are on that
tablet, Isaac Muzzey, was my kinsman. Amos Muzzey, my
grandfather, was a member of that Spartan band commanded
by Parker, the Leonidas of the Revolution. My own father,
born on the 19th of April, saw the British column, a boy of
nine, on that day, and half a century afterward he took the
depositions of five of the survivors of Captain Parker's company, to the effect that they witnessed the return of the British
fire by our soldiers. And, in the recent struggle to save the
life of the republic, out of fourteen of my name and blood, of
the age to bear arms, eleven took part in the contest.

For another reason I rejoice to be with you at this time. The men of my profession took a conspicuous share in our great Revolution. In their preaching and their devotions on the Sabbath, they remembered their country. When President Langdon offered prayer with our troops on Cambridge Common, as they left, in gloom and doubt but with brave hearts, for the bloody struggle of the 17th of June, he followed a custom not uncommon in that eventful period. What Macaulay says of the early Puritans was true of their descendants; seconded and supported by their ministers, they were men " who could look calmly upon the stormy battle, because they had first looked upward to God." To Jonas Clark the pastor of Lexington, it was in large measure owing that this town so early took a bold and decided stand for the rights and liberties of the Colonies. Not only by his appeals in the pulpit, but by his zeal and perseverance in private and in public, by his sound judgment and broad views, he showed himself a statesman, and fitted for a far higher sphere than he ever reached. By his voice and by his pen, he took a prominent part in many measures that led on to the final establishment of our civil and religious rights, and to the independence of these United States.

To Mr. Clark's influence, joined to their own inherent patriotism, it was due that, so early as 1765, the inhabitants of Lexington at a public meeting asserted their chartered rights and privileges, and protested against the odious Stamp act. Nor did they limit their interest to themselves; but in 1768 they chose a delegate to " join," as they expressed it, " such as were, or might be, sent from the several towns in the Province, to consult and advise what may be best for the public good at this critical juncture." In 1769 they passed a vote " not to use any tea or snuff till the duties are taken off." And in 1774, they chose a delegate to the Provincial Congress.

Thus from the beginning was seen the influence of these local municipalities on the destiny of the whole country. In every land, but nowhere more remarkably than in this, it is manifest that the history of towns is a most important part in the history of nations. Towns are only the elements of nations; and whatever affects the well-being of the one, affects that also of the other. John Adams, writing of the situation of beleaguered Boston in 1775, says, " the condition of that beloved town will plead with all America with more irresistible persuasion than angels, trumpet-tongued."

There is a peculiar fitness in combining, as you do this day, the dedication of your "Town and Memorial Hall." The two are inseparably connected. The course pursued by this town, from the inception of the Revolution down to the present day, has been not of local interest alone, but national. The whole country has an equal share in the great system of free, representative institutions, the inauguration of which was insured on this spot the 19th of April, 1775. These memorial tablets record indeed only the names of the sacred band belonging to your own town. But Parker led more than that little company who stood on yonder green; he led the embattled host that partook of his and their spirit thenceforth. When he rallied his men in the afternoon of that signal day, and met the returning enemy, he prefigured our noble army, which, again and again, with thinned ranks and amid fallen comrades, returned to the dread fields of that long and bloody struggle.

"Lexington, in the sacrifice of that day," as our worthy historian tells us, "lost, including all her killed and wounded, both morning and afternoon, more than one-sixth of her entire company,—a proportion greater than that of the most sanguinary battle-fields in all history." Who can be surprised that her illustrious example stirred the entire continent to arms? Who can wonder that no less than twenty cities and towns in the Union have taken her venerated name? Wherever, indeed, the great gospel of liberty shall be made known, this which she hath done, shall be told also for a memorial of her.

I rejoice that the new monument, projected nearly twenty years since, and made the occasion of that eloquent address of Everett to the whole people of the United States, was not lost sight of; but you have combined with its noble purpose the still wider object of a memorial to those of this town who fell in the late civil war. You do well to add the plan of a Public Library. So should it be always: light and liberty, the education of the people, step by step with the extension of our limits and the progress of each age. They were our intelligent yeomanry, freeholders and freemen, who here laid the corner-stone of the republic. They who thought deeply, as well as felt strongly, in the infancy of our freedom, did their part toward

the emancipation of these colonies, no less than the gallant
Parker and the determined men in his command.

They fought for their firesides, but not for them alone. That
was indeed a sad night when the alarm guns were fired and the
drum beat to arms. Dark, indeed, was that day when wives
and mothers and sisters saw those dearest to them go forth, not
knowing the dim future, but sure that some homes must be
made desolate. Stern was the summons to check their tears,
and bind up the bleeding wounds, and speak peace to the dying.
Would that we could do justice to their service and sacrifice.
What better can we do than to ponder their example and imbibe
their spirit? With this "memorial" of the past, we can learn
from them the great lesson that the love of home and the love
of country should be one and indissoluble in our hearts. We
were taught in the recent test of our institutions, for which new
patriot-martyrs, thank God, sprang up, that we are never to rest
on our arms, and feel sure that the country is safe. We may
well to-day, as we look at the alienations and the disuniting
causes and tendencies among portions of the people, and in our
national councils, take up the strain of the elder Quincy, who
died just before our Republic was born, "Now is the time to
summon every aid, human and divine, to exhibit every moral
virtue, and call forth every Christian grace. The wisdom of
the serpent, the innocence of the dove, and the intrepidity of
the lion, with the blessing of God, will save us."

In this home of our fathers, let us drink at the same fountain
of pure patriotism from which the men whose names we here
consign to our children, drank in the day of their perils and
toils, their anxieties and their sacrifices, on to the pouring out of
their life-blood. And may the draught invigorate us for every
high duty we owe to this consecrated soil, the protection of our
domestic altars, the repression of all narrow and selfish purposes, the upholding of our free institutions, and the perpetuity
of the Union.

Eighth regular toast:

Memorial Hall—Devoted to the memory of the martyrs of
liberty and patriotism.

> "Who seem to die in such a cause
> We cannot call them dead."

H

58

Response, " Auld Lang Syne," by the Band.

Ninth regular toast :

The Cary Library—A supplement to the common school, calculated to improve and elevate the community.

Eloquently responded to by Hon. JOSEPH WHITE, Secretary of the State Board of Education.

Tenth regular Toast :

The Soldiers of the late War—Let not the depth of our remembrance of the dead make us forget the claims of the living.

Responded to by Col. JOHN W. HUDSON.

Mr. President:

It is strikingly true of Lexington in one particular, that her experience during the late rebellion was an epitome of that of the nation ; for the officers and men who served on her quota, (and the same is true of those who have, since the war, come here to live,) were to be found in active service in nearly all the departments into which the military forces of the Union were divided, from 1861 to 1865.

Of such of these gentlemen as survive the war I will gladly say a few words, since they are too unassuming to say much about themselves. Indeed, one of them, now resident here and well known to you, Capt. MORSE,* served zealously in the field for two years, and was then so severely wounded in battle that the surgeons despaired of his life ; and yet some of our people were not aware that he had been in the service at all.

Of the experiences of these men, no town need have been ashamed. You have already been told by Gen. CHAMBERLAIN how early one of the CHANDLER† family began his active service. Another‡ (one of the Marshals to-day) enlisted in a militia company about the same time, bore a part, with several comrades from the town, in the first battle of Bull Run, and with one of these§ was wounded and carried away to Libby Prison ; and there CHANDLER was reduced so low and detained so long

* Capt. JOHN N. MORSE, 35th Mass. Vols.
† EDWARD T. CHANDLER, 3d M. V. M.—afterwards 22d Mass. Vols.
‡ SAMUEL E. CHANDLER, 5th M. V. M., and afterwards Adj't of a Mo. Cav. Regt.
§ HENRY A. ANGIER, 5th M. V. M.

that he was given up, at length, for dead, and remarks appropriate to such a supposition were made in one of our churches.

Others, of those still living, participated in the battles of the Peninsula, from Yorktown to Malvern Hill, in the disasters of Pope's Retreat, in the struggles at South Mountain, Antietam, Fredericksburg and Chancellorsville, in the closely contested operations in North and South Carolina, and in the tremendous conflict at Gettysburg; and from the best information I can obtain, they quite uniformly helped sustain the reputation for courage and steadiness of the 12th, 13th, 16th, 22d, 24th, and other regiments, in which they served. One[*] of those present to-day lost an arm in rescuing the colors of the 22d regiment at Gaines' Mills, and received some slight wounds afterwards. At Antietam several of those who survive were severely injured,— one of them, Lieut. DEAN, of the 35th regiment, (also one of the Marshals to-day,) so badly that he has literally been rescued from the jaws of death.

In the assaults made and received by the Army of the Potomac in its long campaign under Gen. Grant, many of these men well sustained their parts at the Wilderness, Spottsylvania, the North Anna, Cold Harbor, the investment of Petersburg, the battle at the Mine, and the incessant extensions of the lines to the left, till at last the enemy's works were taken, and, after a short pursuit of Lee, our labor was done. And then it fell to the lot of Lexington, of all the towns of the loyal States, to furnish the excellent and experienced commissary[†] who was selected out of the whole Army to go over to Appomattox Court House and ration the prisoners there taken and paroled.

At Spottsylvania, where the Second Corps captured the entire division of Bushrod Johnson, some of the soldiers of this town were at the extreme front in that wild scene, one of whom, already distinguished by heroic service in seizing the colors of his regiment just as they had been twice struck down—in which act he was dangerously wounded—and by marked good conduct on all occasions, here actually crowded his way through the enemy at the head of his company, doing probably as good service as any person on that field. I refer to another of the Marshals, Major

[*] Louis E. Crone, now Captain U. S. Army, resident in Lexington.
[†] Major Loring W. Muzzey, A. C. S. Vols.

CAPELLE of the 16th regiment, who left the State a corporal and came home promoted and brevetted for bravery in action.

And a few days later, in a most gallant charge upon two successive lines of works, another of your guests to-day, Major KELIHER,* now of Lexington, was nearly torn in pieces by a shell, so that all I can find of his subsequent experience with his regiment, is the fact that he returned to the front and was honorably discharged for his injuries.

Several times as Grant knocked at the gates of Petersburg, it became necessary, as a part of his plans, to make demonstrations before Richmond. In these demonstrations—nothing less than severe, and, of course, hopeless battles—in the 24th and other regiments, several of the men of whom I am speaking, constantly assisted, and not without adding to already well-earned reputations for distinguished courage.

And let it not be forgotten that one† of your citizens, who served faithfully in the Army of the Potomac, and is also your guest to-day, survives the hardships and fiendish horrors of the Andersonville Prison.

In other parts of the country, too,—in the movements of the army of Buell and Rosecrans,‡ in the capture of New Orleans, the siege of Vicksburg, the defence of Knoxville, and the deliverance of the forces hemmed in at Chattanooga, in the gallant Navy,§ and wherever our arms were borne except, perhaps, the North West, some of these gentlemen sustained their full share of the hardships, the romance and the glory of the grand conflict. One of them, PAGE,‖ (another of your guests,) lost his arm as Hooker's command, to which he belonged, was securing Lookout Mountain, while the rest of the forces near Chattanooga carried Missionary Ridge, and the combined movement opened the way for the capture of Rome and Atlanta, and for the great march to the sea.

And I can testify, from personal observation, of the alacrity with which such services have been performed. For example, while the first movement against the ridge that shielded

* Major JOHN KELIHER, 20th Mass. Vols.
† GEORGE B. DENNETT, 12th Mass. Vols.
‡ Colonel JOHN G. CHANDLER, U. S. A., of Lexington, served in this army.
§ Among others, JOHN WHITMAN, Acting Ensign, U. S. N.
‖ GROVNER A. PAGE, 33d Mass. Vols.

Petersburg, was in progress, I was unexpectedly greeted one afternoon by a young man, a neighbor at home, from the very borders of Lexington Common, and who was then serving in a Massachusetts regiment in the Fifth Corps. I know not why I should conceal the fact that he bore the honored name of HARRINGTON.* He told me it was his brigade, the rear of which was nearly concealed in the woods close by, and that he supposed they were going to charge the rebel position which, he understood, lay beyond. We enjoyed a few minutes' pleasant talk of home and of army affairs, when the bugles in the woods sounded the attention. "My brigade is going in," said he, "those are our bugles;" and with a hasty good-bye, and the outward appearance of as light a heart as if he were bidden to a festival of peace, he seized his musket and disappeared into the woods at the steady double-quick step of the trained soldier. Five minutes later I heard the desultory skirmish fire, and then the rapid and confused sound of musketry, which indicated plainly enough the fact that his brigade had indeed gone in, and was sharply contending for what, I know too well, became from that day forth, historic ground. He survives the war, but not, it would seem, because he shunned its dangers.

Several years ago a quite young man, then resident in town, left our High School and removed to the West, where for a time we lost sight of him. After the war began we heard that he was in the Volunteer Army, and that he was serving as a drummer. He was in the army, an enlisted man, but not a drummer, nor yet a clerk at head-quarters, for which position his penmanship and other acquirements would have fitted him uncommonly well. He was a corporal in the ranks, armed and accoutred with musket and cartridge-box and forty rounds, a member of the 11th Illinois Infantry. He was at Fort Donelson, "hereafter," as Grant's order declared, to "be marked in capitals on the map of our united country." There, after a night of terrible hardship, necessarily passed without fires,—the mercury only ten degrees above zero,—the troops sustained an almost overwhelming attack from the enemy, when at length a general assault was ordered and persisted in till a commanding position was gained, and the fate of the stronghold was

* GEORGE D. HARRINGTON, 22d Mass. Vols.

decided. In this bold and bloody struggle our corporal was so severely wounded that, for more than six months, he was unable to leave his bed. He has a double claim, therefore, to rank with those to whom Grant's order referred in the further words, " and the men who fought the battle will live in the memory of a grateful people." He was honorably discharged for his wounds ; yet even after this experience he did active and useful militia service on the Mississippi so long as such service was needed. He* is now your valued and honored townsman of Lexington, none other than our present Town Clerk.

I have been thus particular, sir, in adverting to the services of the persons to whom the sentiment referred, because I feared that in the attention which we all give to the affairs of the hour, what was already known of the deeds of your own soldiers might be forgotten, and because I believed that, without some such reminder, more than these gentlemen in their modesty would offer, our people would neither know nor conjecture how many of the painful toils and grander scenes of the late great war are represented in the very men whom you have been accustomed to see daily walking your quiet streets.

Eleventh regular toast :

Acton—Her sacrifices on the 19th of April, 1775, show that her patriotism was not confined to her own soil.

Twelfth regular toast :

Arlington—A way-station between Boston and Lexington, where Lord Percy's baggage train was switched off the track.

In answer to the inquiry, What became of Percy's baggage? some one facetiously replied, that Percy got a *check* for it.

Thirteenth regular toast :

The City of Charlestown—She glories with no ignoble pride in the possession within her borders of soil consecrated to liberty.

The following letter from Mayor KENT was read in response :—

* LEONARD G. BABCOCK, Esq.

City of Charlestown, Mayor's Office, April 18, 1871.

HON. CHARLES HUDSON, *Chairman, &c. :—*

Dear Sir.—I have received your invitation to be present to-morrow, on the anniversary of the battle of Lexington. I should be exceedingly gratified to be with you, but my engagements will not admit of it. The city of Charlestown has much in its history and associations, in common with those of your ancient town, and it cannot but sympathize with you on an occasion of so much interest to her as well as to you. If I understand the character of your services, you are to commemorate not only the deeds of the fathers, who died to *achieve* Liberty, but also those of their descendants who died to *preserve* it.

Fitting and right it is, that, on such an Anniversary day, the people should come together, and, as it were, renewedly consecrate the memories of these men. As long as Bunker Hill Monument shall stand—as long as the enduring marble on your Common shall remain—as long as one stone of your Memorial Hall shall rest upon another—as long as the record of great deeds done, shall last—so long let us and our children cherish in all its vital force and essence, that idea, the value of which both the fathers and the sons sealed with their blood—the idea of Liberty under the Law.

Thanking you personally, and in behalf of the city of Charlestown, for the courtesy extended to me,

I have the honor to remain,

Your obedient servant,

WM. H. KENT.

Ex-Mayor ROBINSON of Charlestown, who was called upon, responded in the following eloquent speech :—

Mr. President. I hardly expected to be called on to respond for the City of Charlestown. After the appropriate letter which has just been read from her worthy Mayor, no word of mine is necessary in her behalf. Charlestown needs no one to respond for her. The history of what she has done and suffered in the cause of liberty, is always eloquent, and its remembrance is a fitting response on this occasion. But, Sir, I am proud to speak for her here to-day, and am happy to be present and participate in these memorial services and festivities. Charlestown rejoices with Lexington. Both have much in common; both possess soil on which patriotic men braved death, in order that a nation might live. Lexington is suggestive of Concord and

Bunker Hill,—three noble names which will be remembered and cherished so long as the history of American Independence shall be preserved.

This goodly town has much of which to be proud. She has other honors than that of April 19, 1775. The grandfather of John Hancock—that great patriot of the Revolution—was a minister here for fifty-four years; his father was born in this town, and it almost seems as though he was a child of Lexington. Then, too, it is not unworthy of mention, that the Rev. Jonas Clark was for many years, the venerable and respected minister in this place. He was fitted for the times in which he lived. How much do we, how much did the men of his day owe to him, for the words of patriotism and religion which he uttered in the old meeting-house on the Common. His preaching did much to strengthen and fire the hearts of our patriotic fathers, and enable them to meet with firmness, the day of trial and of blood. I have sometimes thought that the lessons which he taught, and the spirit which animated him were learned and caught by Captain John Parker, the commander of that heroic company who faced the British soldiery on the day which we now commemorate, and, by some subtle process, communicated to his grandson.

Theodore Parker was a son of Lexington. I mention his name with love and respect. Although his religious views may not be accepted, there can be no one so prejudiced as not to honor him for his great, self-sacrificing life—his noble words and efforts in behalf of freedom and the uplifting of his fellowmen. His grandfather, on yonder green, met the enemies of his countrymen, in order to secure liberty for the white man, but his grandson, with a broader love and an universal application of the principles of liberty, contended for the freedom of all. And it is not too much to say, that his labors and efforts contributed in a large degree, to secure the liberation of four millions of slaves. In this place of his birth, let us not be unmindful of his goodness, his purity of life, his devotion to what he believed to be right, and of that independence of spirit which was intolerant of every kind of bondage. Let us keep his memory in sweet remembrance, for he was a worthy descendant of a noble patriot, and a fair fruit of his native soil.

Mr. President, you must excuse me if I become a little exuberant. I am at home again ; every sound is merry, and everything is pleasant :

> " Home, home, sweet, sweet home,
> —— there's no place like home."

I am a boy again, and the by-gone days come back to me. Everything to-day greets me with a familiar face. These fields and hill-sides have been my play-grounds—the neighboring woods have echoed to the sound of my gun—the streams and ponds on the outer limits of the town, have acknowledged the presence of my fishing-rod—and the streets and paths have responded to the footfall of my school-boy feet. I see around me many of my youthful companions and playmates—many others to whom I looked up with respect and confidence—others who warmed my young heart by words of encouragement, and familiar faces greet me on every side.

But alas! As I look about me I miss many well-remembered forms, and my youthful vision vanishes. No, no, I am not a boy again ; there has been a change.

The occasion, however, which has brought us together, recalls me from such thoughts as these, and inspires other emotions and suggests other themes. It is a privilege to be here ; it is also our right and our duty. The sight of the old flag enkindles our patriotic ardor, and the eloquent oration to which we have this day listened, cannot but cause us to appreciate more highly, the blessings of American liberty, and of those institutions which are the safeguards of a free people. Our country has become the home of a great nation ; we all rejoice in her prosperity, and stand proudly erect because of our citizenship. By the great principles of truth, liberty and justice, has she advanced in her honorable career, and taken her place in the front rank of nations, and the day is not far distant when the star-spangled banner shall wave in beauty over the continent, from the North Pole to the Isthmus, as it now does from the Atlantic to the Pacific shores, and the great glory of all shall be, that every one, however humble, and of whatever color, shall stand erect in the freedom of liberty and law, and there shall be none to make him afraid.

1

Sir, I can feelingly respond to the sentiment just offered. I am a native of this town; the family of my father had relatives in the battle of Lexington; my mother is a descendant of the Hosmers of Acton, who, at the old North Bridge in Concord, with their compatriots, met the British foe,

" And fired the shot heard round the world ; "

and until recently, my residence was on the spot over which the red coats passed in their assault at Bunker Hill. These three historic places can glory with each other in the possession of an honorable fame. Each has a record sufficient for itself, and has no cause to disparage that of the other. Surely, Charlestown rejoices with Lexington and Concord in the possession by each of that which is dear to us all; and she cannot more fittingly respond on this occasion than in the expression of the hope that each recurring anniversary of the great events of 1775 will deepen the interest which the people of the three towns have in the welfare of each other, and that the sympathy and good feeling which arise from sufferings in a common cause, will become broader and fraternal, and yearly consecrate anew the soil sacred to the cause of liberty.

Fourteenth regular toast :

The Clergy of our day—They have a shining example in the Lexington pastor of 1775.

Rev. EDWARD G. PORTER responded :—

Mr. President :

I was just leaving the hall when your committee detained me to say a word in reply to this toast. If there were time I would gladly speak of the important services rendered to the cause of patriotism by the eminent men, who, through successive generations, occupied the old Lexington pulpit. This town will never forget the names of HANCOCK and CLARK, whose united ministry extended over the remarkable period of one hundred and five years. They had long pastorates in those days as well as long sermons; and the accounts do not show that the people were weary of either. Some of their sermons have lately come into my hands—quaint looking documents, all worn by use and stained by time. They are written generally in a vigorous, logical style, and show a thorough knowledge of the

Scriptures as well as a deep interest in the events of the time. No one was before the Rev. JONAS CLARK in catching the spirit of freedom, which in the spring of '75 began to spread with such rapidity among the colonists.

If the men of Lexington were ready when the call of duty came, it was because they had long been trained to a high estimate of liberty in civil as in religious matters. In the old "meeting-house," (which I wish were still standing among us, as a memorial of those times,) they often heard strong appeals to stand firm by the principles which they had inherited from the Fathers of New England.

I trust, sir, that with such bright examples before us, the ministry and the citizens of Lexington will ever be true to those lofty and patriotic sentiments which have to-day been repeated in our hearing, and which we are proud to have inscribed upon our Tablets with the names of our honored dead.

This closed the regular toasts of the occasion, but a few voluntary sentiments and speeches were indulged, of which we are able to notice the following :

The Ladies of Lexington :

Offered by Hon. S. B. RINDGE, and responded to by cheers.

Our Generous Benefactress, Mrs. Maria Cary—Many daughters have done virtuously, but thou excellest them all.

Offered by the President of the day, who accompanied the sentiment with a neat speech.

The exercises were brought to a close by a grand ball in the newly dedicated Hall, where the time was pleasantly passed in social greetings of old and new friends and festive enjoyments till the "wee' small hours of the night."

The occasion throughout was one of universal enjoyment, and will be long remembered with pleasure by those who were so fortunate as to participate in it.

APPENDIX.

— —

HISTORICAL SKETCH.

In compiling a Historical Sketch of the inception and completion of the *New Town Hall*, embracing as it does within its walls, a Town Hall especially adapted to municipal purposes and for the public use of citizens, a Memorial Hall, commemorative of great events in national and local history, and a Library Hall, for the accommodation of a Free Public Library,—there is need to refer to various sources, all contributing to the accomplishment of the work just completed. These are the action of the Town, the Lexington Monument Association and Mr. and Mrs. CARY through it, and other endowments, chiefly of Mrs. CARY, to the Library and to the general purposes of the Building.

The matter of improved accommodations for municipal and popular uses, was agitated for several years in the Town, and various plans of enlargement and improvement of the old Hall suggested, and committees appointed from time to time to examine the subject. The desirability of improvement had been for a long time conceded, but no acceptable proposition was submitted until certain proffers of aid from Mrs. CARY were made, which brought the subject before the citizens in a more encouraging aspect. In October, 1869, Mrs. MARIA CARY communicated to the Selectmen a proposal to donate six thousand dollars for the purpose of fitting up a Memorial Hall and Town Library Hall, providing the Town should within three years erect a suitable building for municipal purposes, to embrace in its construction suitable accommodations for those objects. The proposal was laid before the citizens at its annual town-meeting, in November of the same year. The subject was referred to a Committee consisting of Messrs. CHARLES HUDSON, JOHN HASTINGS, SARGENT C. WHICHER, HAMMON REED, LUKE C. CHILDS, WARREN E. RUSSELL and REUBEN W. REED, who were empowered to consult

architects and to procure plans and estimates. The committee
reported at a special town-meeting called for the purpose, January
25th, 1870, submitting plans and estimates and recommending the
purchase of the site and the erection of a new Town Hall in accordance therewith. The report was accepted, its recommendations
adopted, and the same gentlemen constituted a Building Committee
with necessary powers, and provision made for funds to pay the cost.
At the same meeting the proposition of Mrs. CARY was accepted and
the Town Clerk directed to communicate to her the thanks of the
citizens for her generous offer.

The Committee immediately undertook their duties, secured the
site and made contracts, and the work begun. Subsequently, in
April, 1870, a further proposition was received from Mrs. CARY,
increasing her donation in the aggregate to twenty thousand dollars,
whereby ten thousand dollars were secured to the general purposes
of the building, six thousand to the Library, and four thousand to
the Memorial Hall through the Lexington Monument Association.
By this munificent generosity the erection of the Building was so
abundantly provided for that the Town was relieved from what might
have been considered by some a serious financial burden.

THE CARY LIBRARY.

THE origin, progress and present condition of the *Cary Library*
may be stated in brief as follows:—The want of greater facilities
for general reading, being felt in this community, a few individuals in
1866, associated and procured a social Library for the benefit of themselves and their families. But Mrs. MARIA CARY, taking a broader
and more liberal view of the subject, and wishing to extend the benefits
of the Library to all the citizens of her native Town, proposed in 1867,
that if Lexington would establish a *free* Library for the benefit of their
entire population, she would place at their disposal the sum of one
thousand dollars, the interest of which should be appropriated to the
support of the said Library. At a meeting of the inhabitants of
Lexington, legally held April 20, 1868, it was voted to establish a
free Library, to accept the generous offer of Mrs. CARY on the terms
specified by her; and in gratitude to the donor, to give her name to
the Library. The Town at the same meeting constituted the Selectmen, the School Committee, and the settled Clergymen of the Town,
the parties designated by Mrs. CARY as Trustees of her gift, a
Committee to obtain books or money for a Library, and when they
should secure an amount equal to four hundred dollars, they were

empowered, through the Selectmen, to draw one thousand dollars from the Treasury for the purchase of books. The Town also voted to provide a place for the Library, and a person to take charge of the same; and to appropriate forty dollars annually towards replenishing the Library—which with the income of Mrs. Cary's gift, would secure one hundred dollars a year for the repair or purchase of books.

The Farmer's Club, having a good Library of nearly five hundred volumes, generously gave their books to the Town; and the Trustees immediately entered into negotiation with the members of the Social Library then recently formed, the greater part of whom readily gave their shares, and the rest were willing to sell out at cost; so that the Town came in possession of two good Libraries of about eight hundred volumes, at a very moderate cost. The Trustees were also enabled to add about four hundred volumes of new books—making about twelve hundred volumes, when the Library was first opened to the public, which was on the 27th of January, 1868. Within the first three months, there were taken from the Library 1,670 volumes—being conclusive evidence that the institution was duly appreciated by the people.

Soon after the Library was opened to the public, Mr. Benjamin De Forest, a public spirited gentleman boarding in the Town, generously placed in the hands of two of our citizens a check of one hundred dollars, to be expended at their discretion in the purchase of substantial, standard works for the Library. This with the annual expenditure, added about two hundred volumes to the catalogue of books the first year.

Starting under such auspices, the Library has steadily increased by gifts and by purchase, till the present number of volumes is about two thousand; and when the books are removed to the new Hall, we have the offer of from two hundred and fifty to three hundred more. Besides, the generous gift of Mrs. Cary of five thousand dollars to the permanent fund of the Library, will give us an annual income of between four and five hundred dollars to sustain this valuable institution, which reflects so much honor upon the founder, and which promises to prove a lasting blessing to our inhabitants.

THE MEMORIAL HALL.

The *Memorial Hall*, which will always be a point of more or less attraction in our public edifice, is in a certain sense the offspring of the Lexington Monument Association. The impression becoming prevalent, that the Monument on the Common did not comport with modern taste, some of our prominent citizens conceived the idea of superseding it by one more in accordance with the spirit of the age. In 1850 they obtained an act of incorporation, and organized a company, making the venerable JONATHAN HARRINGTON, the last survivor of the battle of Lexington, their President. Their object seems to have been simply to rear a more fashionable Monument in honor of the citizens of Lexington who fell on the 19th of April, 1775. Nothing however was done more than to keep up the organization till 1858, when broader and more liberal views prevailed. It was then perceived, that though the existing Monument was somewhat antiquated in its appearance, it bore the impress and breathed the spirit of the Revolution, and was a fit memorial of the sturdy patriots to whose memory it was erected; and it was resolved to give the proposed enterprise a national character, and erect a Monument commemorative of the opening scene of the Revolutionary drama. To carry forward this idea a successful correspondence was commenced with some of the most distinguished men in the country, which resulted in an organization having Hon. EDWARD EVERETT for President, with Vice Presidents representing every section of the country, and each party in politics. The powers of the corporation were vested in a Board of Directors, residents of Lexington and vicinity.

The general design of a *Minute-man*, placed on a lofty pedestal, was adopted, and distinguished artists were employed to perfect the design and mould the figure. A certificate of Membership, of artistic taste, combining a representation of the Monument and of the battle scene, was engraved, and the necessary measures were adopted to obtain the means to carry forward the enterprise. After expending more than two thousand dollars in these preliminary measures, the flattering prospects of the Association were dispelled by the breaking out of the Rebellion. All efforts were suspended during the war, and on the return of peace almost every city and town had its attention called to some local Monument or memorial in honor of its own fallen patriots.

When the effort was made in 1858 and '59, to give the enterprise a national character, WILLIAM H. CARY, Esq., of Brooklyn, N. Y., one of the Vice Presidents of the Association, and a native of Massachusetts, manifested a lively interest in the undertaking, and, having a summer residence in Lexington, the birth-place of his wife, intimated to some of the officers of the Association that he would render some pecuniary assistance towards the completion of the object. But dying suddenly soon after, he made no provision in behalf of the proposed Monument. But his widow and his heirs knowing his intention, with due respect to his memory and a generous sympathy for the object in view, came forward unsolicited, and offered the Association four thousand dollars in aid of the enterprise, three thousand in land for a site, and one thousand in money when the work should be commenced. But the war, as we have seen, paralyzed the efforts of the Association, and peace found them unable to prosecute their design with any prospect of success.

In this state of things Mrs. CARY, ever interested in the prosperity and honor of the place of her nativity, proposed in behalf of herself and friends, that if the Association would relinquish their claim upon the land, and permit it to be sold, the avails of the sale should be passed over to the Association, and that she would make up the sum to four thousand dollars—the said Association to hold it in trust, till the Town should erect a suitable Memorial Hall, when the sum thus given should be expended in tablets or other suitable emblems in honor of the heroes of the Revolution and of the late war. The Association executed a release of the land, and the money stipulated has been promptly paid over, and is to be expended agreeably to the wish of the donors. The original design of a Minute-man has been adhered to; and the combination of the heroes of the two wars, does equal honor to the memory of those who won our independence, and those who sustained the union of the States.

Thus has the Town been mainly indebted for the means of fitting up the Memorial Hall, to Mrs. CARY and her friends, with the cheerful coöperation and aid of the Lexington Monument Association, through whose efforts means are being obtained to complete the design and fill the remaining niches.

DESCRIPTION OF THE BUILDING.

THE Town Hall is situated on Main Street, and occupies a portion of the lot on which the Lexington House formerly stood, and which was subsequently occupied as a young ladies' school. The structure is an ornate piece of French architecture, presenting four facades to the eye, of two stories in height, surmounted by a double Louvre roof, within which is a third story. In outline of ground-plan the building is a parallelogram, or rectangle, of 95 feet in length by 58 feet in width, built of brick with freestone trimmings. The first story is entered under a portico, located in the centre of the principal facade. The entrance communicates with a staircase-hall of 20 1-2 feet in width by 24 feet in depth, the hall containing the principal staircases in two flights, each six feet in width, reaching to the second or hall story of the building. Flanking the staircase hall on each side are apartments for the Selectmen, Town Clerk, Post Office and other business purposes. The staircase hall communicates immediately with the Memorial Hall, which is situated on the same floor in a central part of the building, and consists of an octagon about nineteen feet in diameter, with four wings or corridors, radiating from it at right angles with each other. Two of these corridors, eight feet wide and nineteen feet long, extend to the walls of the building, where they receive the light of two large windows; the remaining two connect, the one with the staircase hall, as above mentioned, with a width of eleven feet by fourteen, and the other by the same width about eight feet in length, with the Library Hall. The octagon is separated from the corridors only by an arch of about ten feet span and about twelve feet above the floor. On the arch in front, as you approach from the staircase hall, is this inscription :

LEXINGTON
CONSECRATES THIS HALL AND ITS EMBLEMS
TO THE MEMORY OF THE
FOUNDERS AND THE DEFENDERS OF OUR FREE INSTITUTIONS.

The angles between these corridor recesses are cut off, so as to present a face of about six feet, which are finished in niches, in which are four marble pedestals, designed to receive life-size marble statues, two of which are nearly completed, and will soon be placed in position.

The statue to be placed on the left from the entrance, is "The Minute Man of '76," and in the corridor recess to the left is a tablet of Italian marble, framed in beautiful red-veined Lisbon marble, on which is the following inscription :

"THE PLEDGE AND ITS REDEMPTION

RESPONSE OF LEXINGTON TO THE
APPEAL OF BOSTON,
DEC 18, 1773.

"We trust in God that should the state of our affairs require it, we shall be ready to sacrifice our estates, and everything dear in life, yea, and even life itself, in support of the common cause."

NAMES OF THE CITIZENS OF LEXINGTON WHO FELL IN FREEDOMS
CAUSE APRIL 19, 1775.

Ensign ROBERT MUNROE, JONAS PARKER, SAMUEL HADLEY, JOHN BROWN
ISAAC MUZZY, CALEB HARRINGTON, JONATHAN HARRINGTON Jr.
JEDEDIAH MUNROE, JOHN RAYMOND, NATHANIEL WYMAN.

"They poured out their generous blood like water, before they knew whether it would fertilize a land of freedom or bondage."—WEBSTER.

On the right and directly opposite the statue commemorative of the Revolution, stands the statue of "The Union Soldier" of the war of the Rebellion, and a second tablet of like character is placed in the corridor recess near this, with the inscription,

"THE SONS DEFENDED WHAT THE FATHERS WON"

followed by the names of twenty soldiers of Lexington, who lost their lives in the late war.

NAMES OF THE RESIDENTS OF LEXINGTON AND OTHERS SERVING ON HER QUOTA WHO GAVE THEIR LIVES TO THEIR COUNTRY IN THE WAR OF THE REBELLION.

Frederick D. Fiske.	Charles Flagg.
Charles H. Fiske.	Warren Kinnaston.
Benjamin F. Thorn.	John F. Regan.
William D. Coty.	Dennis McMahon.
John Manly.	Thomas H. Earle.
Charles H. Potter.	Timothy Leary.
Charles B. Harrington.	William H. Grover.
Capt. Charles R. Johnson.	Charles Cutler.
John O'Neil.	Edward E. Hatch.
Joseph Simonds.	Charles O. Mezzey.

Both of these statues and tablets are the work of J. G. Batterson, Esq., of Hartford, Conn.

The two remaining niches are designed for marble statues of John Hancock and Samuel Adams, which it is hoped will be filled at no distant day.

Passing from the rotunda, the remainder of the length and width of this story of the building, forms the apartment which is to be occupied as a public library and reading-room. This apartment is 55 feet in length by 44 feet wide, and is to be furnished with all the accommodations and conveniences necessary for the purpose for which it is intended.

The two rear outer corners of this apartment are occupied, one as a librarian's room, of 8 by 16 feet, and the other as a staircase and entry, forming a private entrance from the exterior to the Library and audience hall in the second story.

The second story is mainly devoted to the purposes of an audience hall, the floor area of which is 56 by 70 feet, with a clear height of 24 feet. A stage recess of 34 by 9 feet is flanked by anterooms, respectively 14 by 12 1-2 feet. The hall will seat about seven hundred persons, is amply lighted, and its walls and ceiling are tinted in parti-colors. There are two other anterooms in the front corners of the hall, each 17 by 16 feet, connecting immediately with the hall by sliding doors, which, when opened, would make the whole virtually one apartment.

A mezzanine, or intermediate story, in front and rear of the hall, contains two proscenium boxes, over the two anterooms before mentioned. There are ladies' and gentlemen's dressing-rooms over the two front anterooms. The whole interior of the building is finished in hard wood.

About one-half the roof story is sub-divided into halls and other apartments, to be occupied by the Masonic Fraternity of the town. The remaining half is left unfinished.

From the windows of the audience hall can be seen the spot where on the memorable 19th of April the Lexington farmers gathered to strike the first blow for American independence; and the British troops marched past the spot where this building now stands to encounter them. You can also see the house which was at that time a tavern, where the patriots used to meet for consultation, and further away and just discernible, is the house then occupied by Rev. Jonas Clark, where Adams and Hancock passed the night of the 18th of April preceding the Lexington fight.

The building was erected, from designs prepared by Messrs. Gridley J. F. Bryant and Louis P. Rogers, architects, of Boston, by the Hon. Albert Currier, of Newburyport.

THE Committee to whom was intrusted the preparation and publication of the proceedings at the Dedication of the Town and Memorial Hall, on the 19th of April last, respectfully report to their constituents and fellow citizens, that by causes beyond their control, the publication has been delayed longer than was anticipated: but we believe that the value of the pamphlet has been increased by this delay, as it gave the speakers more time to write out and condense their remarks. Knowing that the exercises of the day met with the warm approbation of the public, the Committee were desirous of preserving them entire, as far as practicable; and consequently we called upon our invited guests who had enlivened our services at the table, to furnish us with the substance of their remarks. Common civility required this at our hands, and we only regret that all the gentlemen did not find it convenient to favor us with a copy of their speeches.

It seemed to be due not only to the character of Lexington, but to the cause of history, and to the gentlemen who had honored us with their presence, that a full report of the proceedings of that day should be put in a form which would be preserved as a part of our local annals. We also deemed it due to those by whose liberality we have been aided in the erection of our edifice, and have been enabled to fit up our Memorial Hall, and our Library, to state briefly the origin of these institutions, that those who come after us may know to whom they are indebted for the blessings they enjoy. We have endeavored to give the public a pamphlet which, in its mechanical execution, will do no discredit to the town. It is no part of our duty to pass upon the merits of the performances of the day. We will only say that we cheerfully present them to the public, and invoke their judgment. Nor need we indulge in words of comment or compliment in regard to the Building, its proportions, arrangements or workmanship; they are subject to your criticism, and to the practical test of your occupancy. May the edifice long serve to cherish good government, patriotism and learning.

Respectfully submitted,

MATTHEW H. MERRIAM,
CHARLES HUDSON,
OLIVER P. MILLS,
Committee of Publication.

www.ingramcontent.com/pod-product-compliance
Lightning Source LLC
Chambersburg PA
CBHW020230090426

42735CB00010B/1629